S0-BSX-359

THE DIARY OF A PUBLIC MAN

THE CAPITOL IN LINCOLN'S TIME

The Diary of

A PUBLIC MAN

And a Page of Political Correspondence

STANTON TO BUCHANAN

———◄•►———

Foreword by
CARL SANDBURG

Prefatory Notes by
F. LAURISTON BULLARD

New Brunswick
RUTGERS UNIVERSITY PRESS
1946

THE LIBRARY
COLBY JUNIOR COLLEGE
NEW LONDON, N. H.

E
440.5
D55

COPYRIGHT, 1946, BY THE
TRUSTEES OF RUTGERS COLLEGE IN NEW JERSEY

COPYRIGHT, 1945, BY THE
ABRAHAM LINCOLN BOOKSHOP

All Rights Reserved

27572

PRINTED IN THE UNITED STATES OF AMERICA

CONTENTS

v

FOREWORD

THIS book, whose main document has slumbered in dusty and worn magazine files for over sixty years, and previous to publication had a secret existence of nearly twenty years, is one of the Civil War classics. It appears now for the first time as a compact unit for ready and convenient use, and not requiring such strict care and zealous guardianship as the yellowed and crackling leaves of the old copies of *The North American Review*. There is this added point, however. Prefixed to the main document is a commentary and analysis which in itself may prove to be a classic. We might even add that the prefatory notes of F. Lauriston Bullard constitute a mystery story of no mean merit, particularly when given a second reading after perusal of the main document.

What gives portent and an atmosphere of tension throughout *The Diary of a Public Man* is its timing, its intimations constantly of that strange hush preceding a hurricane. The days crowded each other and the issues long a matter of dispute, controversy, debate, discussion, commanded action that could no longer be put off in favor of more talk. There was faintly but definitely in the air the smoke of war to come. A variety of pivotal figures in Washington and in New York—the Public Man saw them, talked with them or heard of their talk, on streets, in offices, in hotels. The Public Man had an ear for language, and if by any possibility he invented the lines and fabricated the speeches he put within quotation marks he must be credited not only with an extraordinary fertile imagination but an even more extraordinary familiarity with the American language of that day, both in what was immaculately correct or salty and savory vernacular.

Did Mr. Lincoln at a hotel breakfast in New York hear a remark that he would not meet so many millionaires together at any other table in New York, and thereupon make reply, "Oh, indeed, is that so? Well, that's quite right. I'm a millionaire myself. I got a minority of a million in votes last November"—did it happen? Did Mr. Lincoln at a time when the correct vogue in gloves dictated white, when hundreds of correctly gloved men in the audience wore white over their hands, did Mr. Lincoln then sit in a box at the opera with a pair of huge black kid gloves overhanging the red velvet box front, so that a Southern sympathizer in an opposite box commented, "I think we ought to send some flowers over the way to the undertaker of the Union"—did it happen? The Public Man relates such oddities, which naturally are more than oddities, as being told as having happened, and with an air as though he, the Public Man, accepted them as having happened, and took them as having merit enough to be worth putting down in the diary he kept.

Now for the first time we have this diary prefaced with a stern and relentless inquiry as to its origin, as to how and why on magazine publication the efforts of many shrewd and persistent investigators have failed to work out an identification of the Public Man. This inquiry has also clung fast to the yet more important interrogatory, "Is this testimony credible? Are there circumstances or other witnesses who impeach this witness on valid grounds?'' With relation to these questions, Mr. Bullard has for many years made his personal researches and kept in touch with others having a like interest. It has not been a brief and passing interest with him. He has brooded over his ripened conclusions. Unless some now unexpected fresh clues or new and unforeseen evidence comes to light, it is entirely probable that Mr. Bullard's statement of definite findings can stand as final. He indicates an infinitely delicate margin of possibility that hedges complete acceptance of the diary as trustworthy. For those who seek to inquire rather than to quibble and quip, the book has history and mystery, and as the mother said to the boy sniffing at the breakfast set before him, ''You will either eat it or eat around it.'' To Mr. Bullard for his thoroughness are due thanks. And to Ralph Newman, the proprietor of the Abraham Lincoln Book Shop in Chicago, who originated the publication and the plan of the book, are due felicitations on a worthy enterprise.

CARL SANDBURG

THE DIARY OF A PUBLIC MAN

PREFATORY NOTES

NO more interesting and mystifying serial ever has been published in an American magazine than "The Diary of a Public Man" which ran in *The North American Review* from August through November, 1879. The continuing interest in the "Diary" is due to the vital importance of the period which it purports to cover. The entries range over a few widely separated dates, from December 28, 1860, to March 15, 1861. The diarist seems to have known everybody and to have been a welcome visitor everywhere in Washington and New York. He had an ear for a good story, an eye for a significant gesture, and an apparently indelible memory. The men who were struggling with the enormous problems of that stormy time never would have talked with him so freely as they are represented to have done unless they believed him to have been a man of extensive information and rare discretion. He might write things down, but he would keep his mouth shut.

These records are mystifying because the identity of the anonymous diarist never has been disclosed. The editorial note which precedes the first installment contains all the information which Allen Thorndike Rice, the owner and editor of the *Review,* ever made available to its readers. Inquiries were numerous. Within two or three years of its publication, George Ticknor Curtis, at work on his *Life of James Buchanan,* applied to the editor for the name of the writer, but Mr. Rice declined to reveal it. Subsequent owners and editors have disclaimed all knowledge of any clues that might indicate the authorship. Letters and papers of the persons mentioned in the "Diary" have yielded no information of value and, as any casual reader will readily observe, the diarist took great pains to conceal the names of many of the men with whom he discussed the issues on which the unity of the nation depended. The nationwide curiosity and apprehension with which officialdom and the whole people awaited the disclosure of the policies of the New Man from the West is apparent in nearly all the incidents and conversations which the "Diary" records.

One additional reference to the Public Man was published in the *Review*. In the November, 1879, number appears an article containing several "Unpublished Letters of Mr. Stanton to Mr. Buchanan," under the title, "A Page of Political Correspondence." The allusion occurs in a note accompanying the article. It is somewhat defensive in tone. The editor "hopes that it is no longer necessary for him to assure his readers that he takes part neither with the Trojans nor the Tyrians in any of the various controversies which have so far been evoked from time to time by contributors to these pages." He asks his readers to remember this while reading the "Diary" as well as the Stanton-Buchanan correspondence. The letters in question "were handed to the editor for publication by a distinguished gentleman, who desires that his name may not for the present be made known, and into whose possession they came indirectly from a collection of private papers left by the late President Buchanan." These letters, continues Rice, "bear directly upon the very grave and momentous events" dealt with in the "Diary" in "the present number" of the *Review*. At the time the letters were written, Stanton was "bitterly opposed to Mr. Seward" and was against the Administration, "while the diarist, on the contrary, lived in friendly and familiar relations with Mr. Seward, and was evidently more inclined to support than to assail Mr. Lincoln." So, "the corroborative value of the letters to the diary and of the diary to the letters will be evident." And he affirms that he is transmitting to the public all the light both letters and "Diary" throw on that important epoch "exactly as it comes to him," without assuming in any way either to intensify or to mitigate it.

This amounts to a reiteration of the editorial statement with which the *Review* introduced the "Diary" to the public in the August issue. Many readers must have been demanding information. The office mail would be interesting reading today. The Stanton-Buchanan letters are included in this volume in view of what Mr. Rice had to say about them.

Several well-known Lincoln stories trace back to this "Diary"—the black gloves at the opera, where and why the President-elect called himself a millionaire, the chivalry of Senator Douglas at the inaugural ball. Writers both cautious and careless have used these records, more often without than with any warning that their authenticity is debatable.

It may be unfair to say that the publisher never intended to identify the author. The owner of the *Review* died ten years after the "Diary" appeared. He must have been bound by some compact with the diarist or his representative. The contents imply that the Public Man must have been in his middle years or older. How long did he live after 1879, or had he already passed away? Had he made the editor the sole custodian of his secret? Investigators have reached no definite conclusions as to the amount of editing to which the entries may have been subjected for purposes of concealment. Did the diarist and the editor "salt the mine" with misleading hints designed to throw the sleuths off the trail?

On one point at least all students are in agreement. If this "Diary," so-called, is a forgery, it is one of the best jobs of the kind ever put over on a credulous and undiscriminating public, to say nothing of the historians it may have fooled. It probably contains some anachronisms. A few incidents are open to doubt, at least as to certain of their details. Opinions naturally differ as to the correctness of the sentiments attributed to some of the men quoted. The diarist names seventy-five men outright. Edward L. Pierce, the biographer of Charles Sumner, in an address before the Massachusetts Historical Society in 1896, stated that only one of those who survived at the time of publication is depicted as having been on intimate terms with the diarist. As a matter of fact, there were four such survivors. My list of those who had passed away before 1879 includes forty-seven names, and of the remaining twenty-eight, I am sure of the survival of only twenty-one. Did the writer wait intentionally until, as he supposed, the possibility of successful contradiction had vanished? Would the editor of the *Review* knowingly have participated in a hoax? Was he himself deceived? He must have consented to the elaborate precautions for the protection of the anonymity of the diarist. Or were the numerous blanks merely stage properties? In whatever direction one moves he runs against an interrogation point. Buchanan's biographer challenges one incident as containing only "a very few grains of truth" and de-

6

nounces another as "unauthenticated nonsense." Pierce in his address declared that the "Diary" is to be regarded "as a fiction—nothing more nor less," and he argued the point at some length.

Some historians of established authority have used this material in spite of the mystery which envelopes its origin. We do not know how extensively James Ford Rhodes may have explored the problem, but he used the "Diary"; the citations appear in his *History* on the same pages with references to other sources of unquestioned authenticity. Allen Johnson in 1926 published a work on historical method in which he indicated several of the criteria which must be satisfied for establishing the identity of the Public Man. The process of study used by many students is simple enough. A candidate for the authorship is put forward and the known facts of his career are set over against the internal evidence of the "Diary." Was he in Washington on the days the Public Man was there? And in New York? Could he have met Lincoln in 1848? Was he tall enough to catch Lincoln's measuring eye? Was he interested in the tariff? A score or more of such possible parallels must be considered. Allen Johnson thought the diarist was a Senator. Professor James G. Randall finds "excellent reason" to doubt it. He has written that "after an elaborate elimination and checking" he "has been unable to ascribe the 'Diary' to any individual among the few that survive the sifting." His general conclusion is that "neither the authorship of the famous journal nor its authenticity, which is inseparable from its authorship, is proved beyond the possibility of reasonable doubt." Various Lincolnians have addressed themselves seriously to this quest. They have ransacked newspapers, examined time tables, hunted out old hotel registers, read bales of contemporary correspondence, only to find themselves baffled. There exists the possibility also that the original may not have been in diary form. Somebody's reminiscences may have been recast for publication. We know of course that various incidents described in the "Diary" did take place—the Grinnell breakfast, how Douglas held Lincoln's hat, for example. There are other incidents for which the "Diary" is the only known authority, and whose authenticity we would be delighted to see demonstrated. That this extraordinary journal holds an almost unique place among American records is certainly not due to any lack of research by competent investigators.

For more than three score years these memoranda have been available only in the files of *The North American Review*. The purpose of the present publication is to bring them within easy reach of present-day readers. Numbers of Lincolnians are acquainted with them only through the fragmentary citations which are fairly numerous in works that deal in some detail with the period, and in biographies of Abraham Lincoln. The "Diary" ought to be better known. It is here reproduced exactly in the form in which it was originally offered to the public. There were signs at that time of a renewal of interest in Civil War matters and in the wartime President. The Lamon *Life of Lincoln* had appeared seven years before. The "Diary" helped to usher in what has been called the reminiscence decade. The editor of the magazine made something of a specialty of the publication of Lincoln and Civil War articles. That valuable volume, *Reminiscences of Abraham Lincoln by Distinguished Men of His Time*, edited by Mr. Rice, was published in 1886. In that year also the huge *History* by Nicolay and Hay began its run of four years in *The Century Magazine*. William H. Herndon and Jesse W. Weik published their celebrated *True Story of a Great Life* in 1889. It was in 1895 that Ida M. Tarbell started the flood of Lincoln books by her biographical series in *McClure's Magazine*.

The present writer makes no attempt to identify the Public Man. His duty is to provide material which shall promote the reading of the "Diary" with intelligent pleasure, to paint in a background for the better understanding of its allusions to men and events. The owner of the *Review* was a remarkable young man who was himself in the way of becoming a public man of some eminence at the time of his death almost at the end of his thirty-eighth year. Under his supervision the magazine had become one of the wonders of the day.

If some new investigators are moved by this republication to take the trail, so much the better. But it surely would be a pity for anybody other than Professor Frank Maloy Anderson, long connected with the Historical Department at Dartmouth College, to discover and demonstrate the authorship. He probably knows more about the "Diary" than any other living man. This is the result of his long-continued studies of every detail in the "Diary" itself, and of every conceivable outside source that might yield a clue. In December, 1928, Professor Anderson read an unpublished paper at the annual meeting of the American Historical Association, with the title, "Who Wrote the 'Diary of a Public Man,' Amos Kendall, Chevalier Wyckoff, or X?" in which many of his hearers felt he made out a pretty good case for Kendall. One violates no confidence in reporting that Professor Anderson no longer holds exactly to the view he presented on that occasion. One day—his own word is "presently"—he will have a story to tell of the detective work of a historian which should be fascinating and, as offering a solution of a mystery which has defied all students for many years, will certainly be important.

II

When Allen Thorndike Rice bought *The North American Review,* various journals of the time alluded to him disdainfully as ''a conceited youth of foreign education and foppish ways who would rattle around for a while in the chair of James Russell Lowell.'' It is quite true that the young man had been educated abroad and that he took considerable pains with his personal appearance. It is true also that in the ensuing decade he soared into the sky like a rocket but that at no time did he show any signs of coming down like a stick. People wondered why a man of independent fortune, who might have embarked on a social career, ''gave himself,'' as Gladstone said in 1889, ''to the laborious occupation'' which he had deliberately chosen. No ''minion of the press'' ever worked harder.

There was something strange about his origin also. The day after his death the newspapers were two years in error as to the date of his birth. Both Maryland and Massachusetts claimed him as a native son. There was so much gossip that such a man as George Ticknor Curtis thought it advisable ''to refute . . . some of the scandalous stories about his boyhood.'' There was in fact one sensational, and true, story, an episode in which the boy appeared as the victim—or the beneficiary, as you please—of a daring kidnaping exploit.

A full account of the present writer's search for the date and place of Rice's birth might be considered a chapter in a detective story, although the simple facts, once established, proved quite prosaic. Henry G. Rice, Jr., and Elizabeth Francis Thorndike were married in Newport, Rhode Island, on August 5, 1850. The bridegroom came from a family of standing and "moderate property" in Boston; the bride was a granddaughter of "Old Israel Thorndike," a capitalist and shipping merchant of Beverly and Boston. Their son was born in Boston on June 18, 1851, and baptized the following September as Charles Allen Thorndike Rice. Even before the marriage observant neighbors had noticed that the expectant husband was more in love than was his prospective bride. Mr. Curtis included in his statement, published in 1889, some allusions to the opening of the rift between them which ended in two divorces and the abduction of their son by his mother in defiance of the courts of Massachusetts. For some unknown cause the young mother had left Boston with her boy, and up to 1860 they were always together. In that year Henry Rice, in possession of his son for the first time in years, came to Massachusetts with Allen to spend a few weeks on the rockbound peninsula of Nahant. The mother attempted to obtain "her share" in the custody of the boy by the *habeas corpus* process. Three days after the court's adverse decision, she obtained possession of Allen by capture. Of the four accounts of the kidnaping, the best is that of a playmate who witnessed the crime, Henry Cabot Lodge. Mrs. Rice managed to elude her pursuers and get away to Europe with the lad. She established herself in Germany and there married one of Allen's tutors.

Henry White, long known as a career diplomat in the service of the United States, visited Oxford in 1871 and found there an "intellectual set" of young Americans. Among them were Lloyd Bryce and Allen Thorndike Rice who were enrolled at Christ Church College. Both were hard students. Bryce said that his friend "took the highest possible degrees in the shortest possible time." Allen was much interested in world affairs. With relatives in Paris, he crossed the Channel every little while, and thus it happened that he witnessed at close range some of the important events of the fateful days that followed the capitulation of Sedan. On the afternoon of September 4, 1870, he was whirled in a huge crowd to the Hotel de Ville, and managed to stand within a few feet of Gambetta while the Third Republic was proclaimed to the throng below.

College over, Allen Rice came to the United States and soon made the great stroke of his life, the purchase of *The North American Review.* Bryce quotes him thus: "I set myself to thinking how I could resuscitate the *Review,* and I decided to make it the mouthpiece of both sides of every public question." How well he succeeded was recognized everywhere during his management of the magazine, and should be better known today. He became the most audacious and original of publishers and has been deservedly characterized as the first of modern editors. He promoted the Charnay archaeological expedition to Yucatan, the expense of which was divided between his friend Pierre Lorillard of New York City and the French government. At considerable personal risk he went to Pittsburgh for a first-hand study of the great strike of 1877. In 1884 he acquired a controlling interest in *Le Matin* of Paris. Two years later on short notice he ran for Congress on the Republican ticket in New York City and lost by 527 votes in a district normally Democratic by 8,000. He had been defeated by the treachery of certain Republican district leaders. Declaring that he cared less for his defeat than for the debauchery of the ballot, he brought the case before the County Committee and caused one man to be expelled therefrom. And in the *Review* he crusaded for ballot reform.

In 1889 Allen Rice came before the public as one of the youngest Americans ever to be appointed to a diplomatic post of the first rank. The Department of State, correcting for me the dates erroneously announced in the press, certifies that he was informed of his selection as Envoy Extraordinary and Minister Plenipotentiary at St. Petersburg on April 4, and that he accepted the appointment on April 8. President Harrison at the same time named Robert T. Lincoln as Minister to England and Murat Halstead as Minister to Germany. The papers commented on the fact that Rice possessed one rare qualification; an accomplished linguist, he was a master of the language of diplomacy.

And then, on the eve of sailing for Russia, Rice died. The body was taken to the home of Edward Cooper, whose son-in-law was Lloyd Bryce. Many public men came to the funeral in Grace Church. Among the pallbearers were Vice-President Levi Morton and Walker Blaine, representing his father, the Secretary of State, who was unable to be present; General William T. Sherman and Chauncey M. Depew; Pierre Lorillard and William Waldorf Astor.

The tributes of his friends and fellow-editors justify the opinion that Allen Thorndike Rice—as for years he had signed his name, without the Charles—was at the very least a gifted and unusual man. They all mentioned his ceaseless industry, originality of thought, grace and force of expression. Astor alluded to their horseback ride together up the Hudson to Albany. Edwards Pierrepont emphasized his ''having in a large degree what generally

has been found fatal in the great game of ambitious life,''
how he had begun young without a guide, was a favorite
in society, and believed in his high destiny, and yet nobody toiled more earnestly. Bryce cabled a long testimo-
nial from Paris, in which he reviewed the ''strangely ro-
mantic career'' of his friend, and declared him to have
possessed ''many of the essential elements of greatness.''
Among his friends were such contrasting personalities as
Victor Hugo and General Sherman, Alexander Dumas
and Henry George, William E. Gladstone and Laurence
Oliphant.

III

Alexander H. Everett, eleven years after the founding
of the magazine, and four years before he became its editor, is quoted by its centenary historian as having said in
1826: ''I doubt whether the President of the United States
has a higher trust to be accounted for than the editor of
The North American Review.'' While that opinion represented the extreme notions of a scholar, no informed person in that day doubted the responsibility of such a position for the influencing of public opinion. His younger
and more famous brother, Edward Everett, already had
been editor of the *Review* for more than three years. When
he began, the magazine had a circulation of about five hun-
dred, which by unremitting labor he multiplied by five,
a feat almost as remarkable in that time as that achieved
by the editor who published ''The Diary of a Public Man''
a half-century later. The magazine, however, was not designed for public consumption. Founded by a group of
''cultivated gentlemen'' in Boston, and ''modeled on the
famous quarterlies of Great Britain,'' its prestige was not
appraised in terms of circulation. Its editors were men of

14

scholarly eminence, its contributors were writers of acknowledged distinction, its appeal was limited to the ruling caste. It may well be that one of Allen Thorndike Rice's friends exaggerated but little, if at all, in his broad affirmation that at the time Rice bought the magazine it was "profitable neither to its publishers, editors, nor contributors."

For a comparatively brief span of years, beginning during the Civil War, James Russell Lowell and Charles Eliot Norton were in charge. Lowell was more of a star contributor than an editor. He loved leisure and abominated the grind of the editorial desk. The *Review* printed some of his most durable papers, notably that evaluation of the policy of President Lincoln in which in later years he found much satisfaction. A Boston Brahmin had led the country in the divining of the character and the ability of the Railsplitter. Norton was the first editor to pay more than a dollar a page for contributions. On his retirement in 1868, Professor Ephraim Whitman Gurney of Harvard took over the editorial supervision. Four years later Henry Adams became editor and he chose Henry Cabot Lodge as his assistant. During their regime there was no boom in circulation, but some timely articles were printed, and in recognition of the centenary of American independence they filled the issue for the first quarter of 1876 with a symposium of permanent value.

But something happened late in that year, described by Henry Adams in a note to a personal friend as "a trifling disagreement" on account of which he was going to "get rid" of his editorial duties. The public was not officially informed as to the nature of the unexpected upset beyond the somewhat puzzling notice inserted in the final issue for the year by the publishers. This notice, signed by James

15

R. Osgood & Co., was to the effect that "the editors of the *Review* had retired from its management on account of a difference of opinion with the proprietors as to the political character of this number," but that "rather than cause an indefinite delay in publication, they have allowed the number to retain the form which had been given to it, without, however, committing the *Review* to the opinions expressed therein."

It was an article, published anonymously, but written by Charles Francis Adams, Jr., a brother of the editor, the sentiments of which the owners considered themselves in duty bound to repudiate. The title was "The Independent in the Canvass." That was the year of the Tilden-Hayes election. The author's views were too "irregular" for the proprietors. But both of the Adams brothers were proud of the fact that for the first time since the war the ability of the nation to think intelligently and to vote independently had been challenged, and that they had done the challenging.

This incident was quickly followed by other happenings of importance. A new editor had to be found in a hurry. Julius H. Ward, in an article for the centenary year of the periodical, related that the choice fell to him, but that "before the publishers were ready to make it public, Mr. Allen Thorndike Rice purchased the *Review* and repeated the invitation." Rice, then in his twenty-sixth year, had been looking about for some equipage that might facilitate his progress toward the heights to which he proposed to climb. Why would not the *North American* be a suitable vehicle? He would make it a forum in which anybody who had anything of value to say on any subject of present interest should have a chance to say it. It seemed to him that the periodical literature of the world was due for a process of rejuvenation, that it was failing to satisfy the needs of the time, and that the noted European reviews had fallen into a decline that threatened their existence. It was widely believed when Rice died, and the New York papers published it as a fact, that he bought the *North American* for $3,000. A later editor, in a pamphlet bearing the imprint of the magazine, estimated that it soon was returning to the new owner an annual profit of $50,000. In 1889 the papers were saying that it had become one of the foremost periodicals in the world, with a far greater circulation than any other in Europe or America.

The day after Rice took possession he began to practice his formula. For the first time in its history the *Review* was to be conducted by a man not a Harvard graduate. He moved the venerable institution to New York. Boston never forgave him for that. It was "as if the Bunker Hill monument had walked away," said Arthur Bartlett Maurice. The new helmsman instantly substituted six numbers a year for four, and two years later, in the year in which "The Diary of a Public Man" was running, he made the magazine a monthly. Only so could it be kept in close enough contact with public affairs to deal with current issues while they were fresh in the public mind. Rice sought writers from all over the earth. Each number he filled with articles, always substantial and often brilliant, which could not be overlooked by anyone who would keep abreast of the unfolding of events and who would understand their significance.

Within a year everybody who read at all could see that "the young man in a hurry" was going to be a force to be reckoned with. A discussion of the "Resumption of Specie Payments" set the pattern and the pace for the long succession of debates on controversial questions

17

which was quickly established as a standard feature of the *Review*. The debaters were Hugh McCulloch, a former Secretary of the Treasury; John Sherman, the incumbent Secretary; William D. Kelley, a Republican Congressman; Thomas Ewing, a Democratic Congressman-elect; David A. Wells, a Special Revenue Commissioner; and Joseph S. Ropes, a merchant and financial writer of Boston. A few months later the magazine scored a memorable hit with a thirty-three page article by William E. Gladstone, with the attractive title of "Kin Beyond the Sea."

An enumeration of some of its principal features will serve better than generalizations to illustrate the quality of the periodical during the Rice management. In 1878 the question of "Eternal Punishment" was considered by seven writers. The future Cardinal Gibbons and John Fiske, the evolutionist, were among the group who wrote a few months later on "What Is Inspiration?" It was a bold stroke thus to bring religious subjects into such an arena. No topics were more alive at that time. The revised version of the New Testament was about to be given to a curious public. Liberals were hopeful and conservatives were apprehensive as to what might be the effect of the new rendering on orthodoxy. The old conceptions of the Christian faith were under fire. The *Review* became a tilting ground for jousts in which men and women of all shades of belief and unbelief took part. The climax came when Henry M. Field challenged Robert G. Ingersoll in 1887. "Bob" came right back with a thirty-two page reply. In the ensuing tournament of Ingersoll against all comers, both Gladstone and Cardinal Manning, Archbishop of Westminster, leveled their lances against the redoubtable agnostic; and at the end one Chinese told why he was, and another why he was not, a heathen.

Still more numerous and fully as notable were the symposia on political matters at home and abroad. The most mixed melee was that on the tariff as "The President's Panacea," in which seventeen writers took part in one issue of 1888. Socialism, Labor, Monopoly, Prohibition, were other symposium topics. The list has a very modern look. The editor had a keen eye for possibilities in other lines. Charles Stewart Parnell wrote on Ireland, Wendell Phillips on William Lloyd Garrison, Jefferson Davis on John C. Calhoun. Richard Wagner explained his "Work and Mission." Edison told of the phonograph. Andrew Carnegie discoursed on wealth. It became an honor to get into the *Review*, and many there were of all grades of ability who sought to have their celebrity thus certified.

Allen Rice manifested great interest in matters relating to the Civil War. The war leaders were fast quitting the stage. A Democrat who had not been in the war won the Presidency in 1884. General Grant was skillfully exploited for a third term. For whatever reason, the *Review* contained a cluster of war reminiscences in 1878, followed by papers on the United States Army by James A. Garfield. In all, more than sixty war articles were "ordered in" by this editor who had been educated in England, France, and Germany. Grant and Beauregard wrote of their own campaigns. There were nearly a score of articles about Abraham Lincoln.

William H. Herndon wrote his "Friend Weik" in 1887 that he "once wrote a piece . . . for Mr. Thorndike of the *North American Review*," avowing, as he did so many times in his correspondence, that his purpose was simply

19

"to tell the truth" about Lincoln. He would "convince the people that there was one man in America who dares to tell the truth, who was not writing the life of Lincoln under surveillance," as in the case of Nicolay and Hay whose *History* was running in *The Century Magazine* at that time.

In April, 1886, the magazine contained a paper of nine pages, with thirteen pages of facsimiles, bearing the title, "A Famous Diplomatic Despatch." This was the dispatch of May 21, 1861, by Secretary Seward to Charles Francis Adams, containing the instructions of the United States Government for his conduct of American affairs at his lonely outpost in London. The younger Charles Francis Adams, in his biography of his father, says that the original Seward manuscript was designed to produce, and must inevitably have produced, a foreign war, and that it was Lincoln's intervention that prevented such a calamity. In his book the junior Adams also says that the secret history of this dispatch did not come to light until the publication of the Nicolay and Hay life of Lincoln.

That is a mistake. *The Century Magazine* article, containing their account of this matter, was published, without facsimiles, in July, 1888. Their work did not come out in book form until 1890. But in *The North American Review* in 1886 the whole story was told with complete reproductions of Seward's script and the President's interpolations and excisions. It will be remembered also that under an 1885 copyright there was published in the following year the thick volume of Lincoln *Reminiscences* edited by Allen Rice. Unlisted in the table of contents is an introduction by the editor of sixty-six pages. This is a Lincoln essay of high value. It seems to me that the interest of

Rice in Abraham Lincoln was something more than the professional interest of a publisher.

And then in June, 1889, the *Review* came out with a black-bordered cover. The editor was gone!

Such an outline of his work as owner of a magazine which for years had carried on its cover the line, "Edited by Allen Thorndike Rice," raises anew the question of the authenticity of "The Diary of a Public Man." We know that he did do some ugly things. Harry Thurston Peck in one of his books referred to him as "having published an outrageously personal attack upon Mr. Bayard." It was put out in the issue for January, 1886, as the first of a few "Letters to Public Men" which were signed with a pseudonym as Arthur Richmond. Whoever wrote the attack was a man of ability, but it is unpleasant to see such a magazine, which long before had abandoned the old-time policy of anonymity, resorting to fake signatures. Much worse was the article over the same name denounced by Hugh McCulloch in his autobiographical *Men and Measures*. This was a caustic criticism of James Russell Lowell in which was embedded an excoriation of President Cleveland. Once more this Richmond took the field in January, 1889, in a farewell letter to the Secretary of State, who still was Thomas F. Bayard, in which he charged the Delaware statesman with having blundered egregiously in handling American rights against both Germany and England.

These offenses cannot be extenuated as merely "politics," but still they belong to a different classification than a spurious diary. In these "Letters" all is above-board with the exception of the name of the writer. In the "Diary" numerous names are suppressed in the narration of incidents of high significance. The possibility of a "perfect crime" has to be considered in any study of the records alleged to have been made by the "Public Man." More than one student holds the synthetic production theory.

In his will Mr. Rice bestowed on Lloyd S. Bryce "51/100 of my estate and interest of and in *The North American Review*," with the machinery and plant complete. Thus, said a contemporary, "a pronounced young Republican politician willingly bestowed upon a pronounced young Democratic politician the control and editorship of the magazine most conspicuously devoted to the discussion of American political affairs." Both men, however, had "a fine independence of all factional and sectional spirit."

IV

As published in the *Review* this "Diary" has entries for only twenty-one days, although the interval between the first entry and the last is seventy-eight days. Perhaps we have only fragments of what may have been a comprehensive narrative for the whole period, the jottings day by day of an observer who was qualified to confer with prominent politicians and eminent private citizens respecting the complex elements of a problem for which no peaceful solution seemed to be possible. The editor in the brief statement in which he introduced the "Diary" said that he was publishing "a series of extracts" from a record the whole of which he was "not permitted to make public." As to his basis of selection, one guess is about as good as another. A diarist is not a historian, although he may furnish historians with materials of great value. He may or may not undertake to explain the whys and wherefores

22

of the happenings he sets down. Diaries of much value often are simply chronological accounts of what the writer sees and hears.

Such an account will mean much or little to its readers after the lapse of years depending on their familiarity with the period. This "Diary" is as interesting today as ever it was, in spite of the devices employed to conceal certain fundamental facts which a real historian looks for. As Allen Rice said, the "Diary" brings the reader "face to face, as it were, with the doubts, the fears, the hopes, the passions, and the intrigues through which the great crisis of 1861 was reached."

The value of an authentic contemporaneous report, recounting with scrupulous fidelity the intimate conversations and fluctuating rumors of such a period, and these recorded by such a man of affairs as this Public Man appears to have been, is obviously beyond computation. We would gladly accept this "Diary" as a genuine historical document. And still—the doubt remains. This doubt must be removed before this document can be received in full standing among the historical sources on which we depend for our comprehension of the forces which brought about the great Civil War. And, if this "Diary" is in fact a fake, it has full right to be pronounced an—almost—perfect crime.

V

As a handy aid for its reading, whether for pleasure or for serious study, there is here presented a brief outline of events which may serve as a frame-work within which to fit the "Diary." An identifying list of the men who are actually named in the "Diary" will be found on page 129.

1860

Nov. 6 Abraham Lincoln elected President of the United States. In ten of the thirty-three States composing the Union he does not receive a single vote.

Nov. 17 Gustave Koerner of Belleville, Illinois, a former Lieutenant-Governor of the State, has an interview with Lincoln who says he "has no idea of taking a position towards the South which might be considered a sort of apology for his election."

Nov. 21 Lincoln meets Hannibal Hamlin in Chicago and begins a series of consultations over the formation of his Cabinet. These last until his inauguration. In the discussions Lyman Trumbull takes a leading part.

Nov. 27 Lincoln writes to Hamlin that "strong and unexpected" demands have been made for the appointment of Simon Cameron as the Pennsylvania member of his Cabinet.

Nov. 29 George G. Fogg of New Hampshire, Secretary of the Republican National Committee, arrives in Springfield for the first of several conferences with the President-elect.

Dec. 3 Joshua R. Giddings, the militant Ohio Abolitionist, has a long interview with Lincoln.

Dec. 4 President Buchanan's annual message is read in the two Houses of Congress. He holds that the South has no constitutional right to secede from the Union.

Dec. 6 A House Committee of Thirty-three, one Representative from each State, is appointed by the Speaker to deal with the issues between the South and the North.

Dec. 8 Lincoln sends Hamlin a letter for delivery to William H. Seward in which he says: "With your permission I shall at the proper time nominate you to the Senate as Secretary of State for the United States.''

Dec. 11 Francis P. Blair, Jr., confers with Lincoln in Springfield.

Dec. 12 Lewis Cass resigns as Secretary of State.

Dec. 15 Edward Bates of Missouri spends the day with the President-elect.

Dec. 18 Kentucky's Senator John J. Crittenden offers the resolution embodying a group of statutes and constitutional amendments known as the Crittenden Compromise. The Vice-President appoints a Special Committee of Thirteen to take charge of the resolution.

Dec. 20 The South Carolina Convention passes an Ordinance of Secession.

Dec. 24 Edward D. Baker and David Wilmot confer with Lincoln.

Dec. 27 The South Carolina Commission, appointed to ''negotiate'' with the United States for the surrender of government properties in that State, arrives in Washington and learns that Major Anderson had secretly removed his troops on the night of the 26th from Fort Moultrie to Fort Sumter.

Dec. 28 The South Carolina Commissioners have a tense interview with President Buchanan who denies their demands and refuses to order Anderson back to Moultrie. Seward writes a note accepting the Cabinet post.

Dec. 29 Secretary of War John B. Floyd resigns and is succeeded by Joseph Holt.

Dec. 30 Simon Cameron and Edward Bates consult with Lincoln.

Dec. 31 Lincoln writes Cameron that he intends to nominate him as Secretary of the Treasury or as Secretary of War. In a brief note he summons Salmon P. Chase to

Springfield. The Committee of Thirteen reports "inability to agree." Judah P. Benjamin, in a dramatic scene in the Senate, declares the North can "never subjugate the South —Never! Never!"

1861

Jan. 3 Georgia seizes Fort Pulaski at Savannah. Crittenden proposes that his plan of compromise be submitted to a vote of the people; it never comes to a vote in the Senate.

Jan. 4 Chase arrives in Springfield. Alabama takes possession of Fort Morgan at Mobile.

Jan. 6 Norman B. Judd and Gustave Koerner confer with Lincoln on the Cameron appointment. A great anti-secession demonstration takes place in Chicago.

Jan. 7 Florida seizes Fort Marion at St. Augustine.

Jan. 8 Jacob Thompson of Mississippi, Secretary of the Interior, quits the Cabinet.

Jan. 9 Mississippi secedes from the Union. The *Star of the West,* bringing arms and ammunition for Fort Sumter, is fired upon by South Carolina batteries.

Jan. 10 Florida secedes.

Jan. 11 Alabama secedes. New York legislature adopts strong Union resolutions.

Jan. 12 Florida seizes Forts Barancas and McRae at Pensacola.

Jan. 16 George Opdyke and Hiram Barney visit Springfield. After a series of votes the Senate practically "kills" the Crittenden Compromise.

Jan. 18 The Massachusetts General Court declares that South Carolina has gone to war.

Jan. 19 Georgia secedes.

Jan. 21 Jefferson Davis makes his farewell speech

to the Senate. In a Boston speech Wendell Phillips advocates allowing all the slave states to leave the Union. A Senate vote, 36 to 16, completes action for the admission of Kansas as a state.

Jan. 24 Georgia seizes the United States arsenal at Augusta.

Jan. 26 Louisiana secedes.

Jan. 29 When a United States Treasury official reports himself unable to prevent the seizure of the revenue cutters at Mobile and New Orleans, Secretary of the Treasury John A. Dix wires in reply: ''If anyone attempts to haul down the American flag shoot him on the spot.''

Feb. 1 Texas passes a Secession Ordinance to be voted upon by the people on the 23rd.

Feb. 4 Delegates from six states meet at Montgomery, Alabama, to form a ''Congress of Sovereign and Independent States.'' A Peace Convention representing twenty-one states, called on the initiative of the General Assembly of Virginia, meets in Washington.

Feb. 5 Horace Greeley confers with Lincoln in Springfield.

Feb. 8 The Montgomery Convention unanimously adopts a Constitution.

Feb. 9 Jefferson Davis and Alexander H. Stephens are elected Provisional President and Vice-President of the Confederate States of America.

Feb. 11 Lincoln leaves Springfield for Washington.

Feb. 18 Davis and Stephens are inaugurated at Montgomery.

Feb. 19 Lincoln arrives in New York and confers with various committees.

Feb. 21 Confederate Congress confirms Robert Toombs as Secretary of State, Christopher Memminger as Secretary of the Treasury, and L. P. Walker as Secretary of War.

Feb. 23 Lincoln arrives in Washington after a secret journey from Harrisburg through Baltimore. The Texas vote ratifies secession 35,000 to 11,000. Lincoln calls on President Buchanan.

Feb. 25 The President calls on the President-elect. Lincoln with Seward visits the Supreme Court and the two Houses of Congress.

Feb. 27 The Peace Convention submits to the Senate a constitutional amendment of seven sections.

Feb. 28 The House by the necessary two-thirds vote adopts a proposed constitutional amendment that "no amendment shall be made to the Constitution which will . . . abolish or interfere with the domestic institutions" of any state "including that of persons held to labor or service by the laws of said State."

March 2 The Senate, 24 to 12, adopts the proposed amendment. Only three states ever ratified it.

March 4 Abraham Lincoln is inaugurated as President of the United States.

March 5 Dispatches from Major Anderson advise that his food supply is running short and that a fleet and an army of 20,000 men would be necessary to "raise the siege" of Fort Sumter.

March 15 All but two members of the Cabinet advise the abandonment of Fort Sumter.

April 8 President Lincoln orders a relief expedition sent to the fort.

April 12 The Confederates fire on Fort Sumter and the Civil War begins.

F. LAURISTON BULLARD

THE DIARY OF A PUBLIC MAN

UNPUBLISHED PASSAGES OF THE SECRET HISTORY OF THE AMERICAN CIVIL WAR

EDITOR'S NOTE

As a contribution to what may be called the interior history of the American Civil War, the editor of the "North American Review" takes great pleasure in laying before his readers a series of extracts from the diary of a public man intimately connected with the political movement of those dark and troubled times. He is not permitted to make public the whole of this diary, and he has confined his own editorial supervision of it to formulating under proper and expressive headings the incidents and events referred to in the extracts which have been put at his service. When men still living, but not now in the arena of politics, are referred to, it has been thought best to omit their names, save in two or three cases which will explain themselves; and, in regard to all that is set down in the diary, the editor has a firm conviction that the author of it was actuated by a single desire to state things as they were, or at least as he had reason at the time to believe that they were. Those who are most familiar with the true and intimate history of the exciting times covered by this diary will be the most competent judges of the general fidelity and accuracy of this picture of them; nor can it be without profit for the young men of the present generation to be thus brought face to face, as it were, with the doubts, the fears, the hopes, the passions, and the intrigues through which the great crisis of 1861 was reached. It is always a matter of extreme delicacy to decide upon the proper moment at which private memorials of great political epochs should see the light. If there is danger by a premature publicity of wounding feelings which should be sacred, there is danger also in delaying such publications until all those who figured on the stage of political affairs have passed away, and no voice can be lifted to correct or to complete the tales told in their pages. In this instance it is hoped that both of these perils have been avoided. While many of the leading personages whose individual tendencies, ideas, or interest, gravely and decisively affected the cause of American history just before and throughout the Civil War are now no more, many others survive to criticise with intelligence and to elucidate with authority the views and the judgments recorded in this diary from day to day under the stress of each day's crowding story. — EDITOR.

ALLEN THORNDIKE RICE

THE DIARY OF A PUBLIC MAN

PRESIDENT BUCHANAN AND SOUTH CAROLINA

Washington, December 28, 1860. A long conversation this
evening with Mr. Orr, who called on me, which leaves me
more than anxious about the situation. He assures me that
he and his colleagues received the most positive assurances
to-day from President Buchanan that he would receive
them and confer with them, and that these assurances were
given them by Mr. B——, who certainly holds the most
confidential relations with the President, not only as an
editor of the official paper but personally. He declared to
Mr. Orr that Anderson's movement from Moultrie to Sumter was entirely without orders from Washington, and offered to bring him into communication with Mr. Floyd on
that point, which offer Mr. Orr very properly declined, on
the ground that he represented a "foreign state," and
could not assume to get at the actions and purposes of the
United States Government through any public officer in a
private way, but must be first regularly recognized by the
head of the United States Government. He said this so
seriously that I repressed the inclination to smile which
involuntarily rose in me. I have known Mr. Orr so long
and like him so much that I am almost equally loath to
think him capable of playing a comedy part in such a matter as this, and of really believing in the possibility of the
wild scheme upon which the secession of South Carolina
seems to have been projected and carried out. He abso-

31

lutely insists that he sees no constitutional reason why the Federal Government should refuse to recognize the withdrawal of South Carolina from the Union, since the recognition of the Federal Government by South Carolina is conceded to have been essential to the establishment of that Government. He brought up the old cases of North Carolina and Rhode Island, and put at me, with an air of expected triumph, the question, "If Massachusetts had acted on the express language of Josiah Quincy at the time of the acquisition of Louisiana, declaring the Constitution abolished by that acquisition, what legal authority would there have been in the Executive of the United States to declare Massachusetts in rebellion and march troops to reduce her?" I tried to make him see that the cases were not analogous, but without effect, nor could I bring him to admit my point that the provision made in the Constitution for the regulation of Congressional elections in the several States by Congress itself, in case any State should refuse or neglect to ordain regulations for such elections, carried with it the concession to the Federal Government of an implied power to prevent any particular State from invalidating the general compact by a failure to fulfill its particular obligations. He intimated to me that for his own part he would be perfectly willing to let the claim of the United States over the Federal property in South Carolina be adjudicated by the Supreme Court, under a special convention to that effect between South Carolina and the United States, after the President had recognized the action by which South Carolina withdrew her "delegations of sovereignty" to the Federal Government. He was careful to impress on me, however, that this was simply his own personal disposition, and not his disposition as a Commissioner.

32

All this was but incidental to his main object in calling on me, which was to urge my coöperation with Mr. Seward to strengthen the hands of the President in ordering Major Anderson back at once to Fort Moultrie. He explained to me that, by this unauthorized transfer of his small force to Fort Sumter, Anderson had immensely strengthened the war secessionists, not only in South Carolina but in other States, who were loudly proclaiming it as unanswerable evidence of an intention on the part of the United States to coerce South Carolina, and to take the initiative in plunging the country into a horrible civil strife, which would be sure to divide the North, and in which the West would eventually find itself on the side of the South. He had seen Mr. Seward during the day, who had fully agreed with him that Anderson's movement was a most unfortunate one, and had suggested that the matter might be arranged if South Carolina would evacuate Fort Moultrie and allow Anderson to reoccupy that post, both parties agreeing that Fort Sumter should not be occupied at all by either. This would, in fact, Mr. Orr said, be conceding almost everything to the United States, as Sumter could not be held against a sea force, and Moultrie commands the town. His explanation of Anderson's movement is that he lost his head over the excitement of two or three of his younger officers, who were not very sensible, and who had got themselves into hot water on shore with some of the brawling and silly young Sea Island bloods of Charleston. As to the willingness of South Carolina to come into such an arrangement of course he could not speak, though he did not believe that Moultrie would have been occupied to-day excepting to afford a basis for it. I agreed with him that anything which could properly be done to avert an armed collision between the forces of the

33

THE LIBRARY
COLBY JUNIOR COLLEGE
NEW LONDON, N. H.

27572

United States and those of any State, in the present troubled and alarmed condition of the public mind, ought to be done; but I frankly told him I did not believe Mr. Buchanan would take the responsibility of ordering Anderson to evacuate Fort Sumter and return to Fort Moultrie, and asked him what reason, if any, he had to think otherwise. He hesitated a little, and finally told me that Mr. Seward had given him reason to think the decision could be brought about through the influence of Senator — —, whose term expires in March, but who has great personal weight with the President, and, as a Southern man by birth and a pronounced Breckinridge Democrat, no inconsiderable hold upon the more extreme Southern men, particularly of the Gulf States. Mr. Seward, in fact, told him that the subject had been discussed by him with this gentleman last night pretty fully, and that he thought Mr. Buchanan could be led to see that the crisis was an imminent one, and must be dealt with decisively at once.

SOUTH CAROLINA NOT IN FAVOR
OF A CONFEDERACY

For his own part, Mr. Orr admitted that he deprecated above all things any course of action which would strengthen the Confederate party in South Carolina. He did not wish to see a Confederate States government formed, because he regarded it—and there I agreed with him—as sure to put new obstacles in the way of the final adjustment so imperatively necessary to the well-being of all sections of the country. He thought that if the United States Government would at once adjust the Fort Sumter difficulty, and recognize the secession of South Carolina as an accomplished fact within the purview of the Constitution, the Independent party, as he called it, in South Carolina would at once come forward and check the now growing drift toward a new Confederacy. The most earnest and best heads in South Carolina, he said, had no wish to see the State linked too closely with the great cotton-growing Gulf States, which had already "sucked so much of her blood." They looked to the central West and the upper Mississippi and Ohio region as the railway history of the State indicated, and would not be displeased if the State would be let entirely alone, as Rhode Island tried to be at the time when the Constitution was formed. In short, he pretty plainly admitted that South Carolina was more annoyed than gratified by the eagerness of Georgia and the Gulf States to follow her lead, and that nothing but the threatening attitude given to the United States by such acts as the occupation of Fort Sumter could determine the victory in that State of the Confederate over the Independent movement.

I could not listen to Mr. Orr without a feeling of sympathy, for it was plain to me that he was honestly trying to make the best of what he felt to be a wretched business, and that at heart he was as good a Union man as anybody in Connecticut or New York. But when I asked him whether South Carolina, in case her absolute independence could be established, would not at once proceed to make herself a free State, and whether, wedged into the Gulf and the middle West as she is, she would not make any protective system adopted by the rest of the country a failure, he could not answer in the negative. He got away from the point pretty smartly though, by asking me whether a free-trade policy adopted from South Carolina to the Mexican border would not be a harder blow at our Whig system than a free-trade policy confined to South Carolina. I asked him whether Governor Pickens, who seems, from what Mr. Orr told me—there is absolutely nothing trustworthy in the papers about it—to have ordered the occupation of Moultrie and Fort Pinckney, is really in sympathy with the secession movement. He smiled, and asked me if I knew Mrs. Pickens. "Mrs. Pickens, you may be sure," he said, "would not be well pleased to represent a petty republic abroad. But I suppose you know," he went on, "that Pickens is the man who was born insensible to fear. I don't think he is likely to oppose any reasonable settlement, but he will never originate one." One of Mr. Orr's colleagues, whom I did not think it necessary or desirable to see, came for him and took him away in a carriage. Almost his last words were, "You may be perfectly sure that we shall be received and treated with."

SENATOR DOUGLAS ON BUCHANAN AND LINCOLN

He had hardly gone before Mr. Douglas called, in a state of some excitement. He had a story, the origin of which he would not give me, but which, he said, he believed: that Anderson's movement was preconcerted through one Doubleday, an officer, as I understood him, of the garrison, with "Ben Wade," and was intended to make a pacific settlement of the questions at issue impossible. I tried to reason him out of this idea, but he clung to and dwelt on it till he suddenly and unconsciously gave me the cue to his object in bringing it to me by saying: "Mind, I don't for a moment suspect Lincoln of any part in this. Nobody knows Abe Lincoln better than I do, and he is not capable of such an act. Besides, it is quite incompatible with what I have heard from him"—he had said, when he checked himself with a little embarrassment, I thought, and went on—"what I have heard of his programme. A collision and civil war will be fatal to his Administration and to him, and he knows it—he knows it," Mr. Douglas repeated with much emphasis. "But Wade and that gang are infuriated at Seward's coming into the Cabinet, and their object is to make it impossible for Lincoln to bring him into it. I think, as a friend of Seward's, you ought to understand this."

I thanked him, but put the matter off with some slight remark, and, without giving him my authority, asked him if he thought it likely Mr. Buchanan would receive the South Carolina Commissioners. "Never, sir! never," he exclaimed, his eyes flashing as he spoke. "He will never dare to do that, sir!" "What, not if he has given them to understand that he will?" I replied. "Most certainly not, if he has given them to understand that he will. That would make it perfectly certain, sir, perfectly certain!" He then launched out into a kind of tirade on Mr. Buchanan's duplicity and cowardice. I tried to check the torrent by dropping a remark that I had merely heard a rumor of the President's intentions, but that was only pouring oil on the flames. "If there is such a rumor afoot," he said, "it was put afoot by him, sir; by his own express proceeding, you may be sure. He likes to have people deceived in him—he enjoys treachery, sir, enjoys it as other men do a good cigar—he likes to sniff it up, sir, to relish it!" He finally cooled off with a story of his having got a political secret out about the Kansas-Nebraska business, which he wished propagated without caring to propagate it himself, or have his friends do so, by the simple expedient of sending a person to tell it to the President, after first getting his word on no account to mention it to any one. "Within six hours, sir, within

37

six hours," he exclaimed, "it was all over Washington, as I knew it would be!"

SECRETARY FLOYD AND THE PLOT TO ABDUCT BUCHANAN

Washington, December 29th. This resignation of Floyd is of ill-omen for the speedy pacification of matters, as he would hardly have deprived Virginia of a seat in the Cabinet at this moment if he thought the corner could be turned. He is not a man of much account personally, and is, I believe, of desperate fortunes, at least such is the current rumor here; but it was of considerable importance that the post he held should be held by a Southern man at this juncture, if only to satisfy the country that South Carolina does not at all represent the South as a body in her movement, and his withdrawal at this moment, taken in conjunction with the lawless proceedings at Pittsburg the other day, will be sure to be interpreted by the mischief-makers as signifying exactly the contrary. The effects of all this upon our trade at this season of the year are already more disastrous than I can bear to think of. My letters from home grow worse and worse every week. No sort of progress is making in Congress meanwhile. B— — has just left me after half an hour of interesting talk. He shares my views as to the effect of Floyd's withdrawal; but a little to my surprise, I own, has no doubt that Floyd is a strong secessionist, though not of the wilder sort, and founds this opinion of him on a most extraordinary story, for the truth of which he vouches. Certainly Wigfall has the eye of a man capable of anything— "The eye of an old sea-rover," as Mary G— — describes it, but it staggers me to think of his contriving such a scheme as B— — sets forth to me. On Mr. Cushing's return

38

from Columbia the other day, *re infecta*, Wigfall (who, by the way, as I had forgotten till B — — reminded me of it, is a South Carolinian by birth) called together a few "choice spirits," and proposed that President Buchanan should be kidnapped at once, and carried off to a secure place, which had been indicated to him by some persons in his confidence. This would call Mr. Breckinridge at once into the Executive chair, and, under the acting-Presidency of Mr. Breckinridge, Wigfall's theory was, the whole South would feel secure against being "trapped into a war." He was entirely in earnest, according to B — — 's informant — whose name B — — did not give me, though he did tell me that he could not have put more faith in the story had it come to him from Wigfall himself — and had fully prepared his plans. All that he needed was to be sure of certain details as to the opportunity of getting safely out of Washington with his prisoner, and so on, and for these he needed the coöperation of Floyd.

He went to Floyd's house — on Christmas night, I think B — — said — with one companion to make this strange proposal, which takes one back to the "good old days" of the Scottish Stuarts, and there, in the basement room, Floyd's usual cozy corner, set it forth and contended for it earnestly, quite losing his temper at last when Floyd positively refused to connive in any way at the performance. "Upon my word," said B — —, when he had got through with his strange story, "I am not sure, do you know, that Wigfall's solution wouldn't have been a good one, for then we should have known where we are; and now where are we?" He agrees with Mr. Douglas in thinking that President Buchanan probably has given the South Carolina Commissioners to understand that he will receive them, and also that he as certainly will not receive them.

39

That mission of Cushing's was a most mischievously foolish performance, and he was the last man in the whole world to whom such a piece of work ought to have been confided, if it was to have been undertaken at all. After sending Cushing to her Convention to treat and make terms, it will be difficult for the President to make South Carolina or anybody else understand why he should not at least receive her Commissioners. It is this perpetual putting of each side in a false light toward the other which has brought us where we are, and, I much fear, may carry us on to worse things. B—— has seen Cushing since he got back, and tells me he never saw a man who showed clearer traces of having been broken down by sheer fright. "He is the boldest man within four walls, and the greatest coward out of doors," said B——, "that I ever knew in my life!" His description, from Cushing's account, of the people of Charleston, and the state of mind they are in, was at once comical and alarming in the highest degree. Certainly, nothing approaching to it can exist anywhere else in the country, or, I suspect, out of pandemonium.

WERE THE CAROLINIANS CHEATED?

January 1st. I took the liberty of sending to-day to Mr. Orr, who brought me the story about President Buchanan's intentions toward the South Carolina Commissioners, to ask him what he thought now of his informant. To my surprise, he tells me that Mr. B——, whom I had supposed to be entirely devoted to the personal interests of the President, persists in his original story, and either is or affects to be excessively irritated at the position in which he has now been placed. Mr. Orr wishes the Commissioners to go home and make their report, but his colleagues insist upon sending in a letter to the President, which I fear will not mend matters at all; and which certainly must add to the difficulty about that wretched Fort Sumter, notwithstanding the singular confidence which Mr. Seward seems to feel in his own ability ultimately to secure a satisfactory arrangement of that affair by means quite outside of the operations of the present Government, whatever those means may be. The South Carolina Commissioners profess to have positive information from New York that the President has ordered reënforcements to be sent to Sumter, and they are convinced, accordingly, that he has been trifling with them simply to gain time for perfecting what they describe as a policy of aggression.

WAS THE CONFEDERACY MEANT TO BE PERMANENT?

January 13th. A very long and interesting conversation with Senator Benjamin on the right of Louisiana to seize Federal posts within her territory without even going through the formality of a secession. He is too able and clear-headed a man not to feel how monstrous and indefensible such action is, but he evidently feels the ground giving way under him, and is but a child in the grasp of his colleague, who, though not to be compared with him intellectually, has all that he lacks in the way of consistency of purpose and strength of will. Virginia, he is convinced, will not join the secession movement on any terms, but will play the chief part in bringing about the final readjustment.

My own letters from Richmond are to the same tenor. After a while I told him what I had heard yesterday from Mr. Aspinwall, whom it seems he knows very well, and

41

offered to read him the remarkable letter from Mr. Aspinwall's lawyer, a copy of which Mr. Aspinwall, at my request, was so good as to leave with me. It illustrates Benjamin's alertness and accuracy of mind that before he had heard six sentences of the letter read he interrupted me with a smile, saying: "You need not tell me who wrote that letter, Mr.— —. I recognize the style of my excellent friend Mr. B— —, of New York, and I can tell you what he goes on to say." Which he accordingly proceeded to do, to my great surprise, with most extraordinary correctness and precision. In fact, I inferred necessarily that the views expressed by Mr. Aspinwall's counsel must have been largely drawn from Mr. Benjamin himself, so completely do they tally with his own diagnosis of the position, which is, curiously enough, that the leaders of the inchoate Confederacy are no more at one in their ultimate plans and purposes than, according to my best information, are the leaders in South Carolina. Mr. Benjamin thinks that the ablest of them really regard the experiment of a new Confederation as an effectual means of bringing the conservative masses of the Northern people to realize the necessity of revising radically the instrument of union. In his judgment, the Constitution of 1789 has outlived its usefulness. Not only must new and definite barriers be erected to check the play of the passions and opinions of one great section upon the interests and the rights of another great section, but the conditions under which the Presidency is created and held must be changed. The Presidential term must be longer, the President must cease to be reëligible, and a class of Government functionaries, to hold their places during good behavior, must be called into being. I could detect, I thought, in his views on these points, a distinctly French turn of thought, but much that he said struck me as eminently sound and sagacious. He thinks not otherwise nor any better of President Buchanan than Mr. Douglas, though his opinion of Mr. Douglas is anything but flattering.

He agrees with me that, by permitting the South Carolina forces to drive off by force the Star of the West, the Government have practically conceded to South Carolina all that she claims in the way of sovereignty, though he is not surprised, as I own I am, at the indifference, not to say apathy, with which this overt defiance to the Federal authority and this positive insult to the Federal flag have been received by the people of the North and West. Certainly, since we are not at this moment in the blaze of civil war, there would seem to be little reason to fear that we shall be overtaken by it at all. The chief peril seems to me now to lie in the long period of business prostration with which we are threatened, especially if Mr. Benjamin's views are correct. I do not believe that his Confederate Government will lose the opportunity of establishing its free-trade system wherever its authority can extend while conducting negotiations for a new organization of the Union, and irreparable damage may in this way be done our great manufacturing interests before any adjustment can be reached.

SEWARD AND VIRGINIA

February 8, 1861. I can anticipate nothing from the Peace Convention. The Virginians are driving things, as I told Mr. Seddon to-day, much too vehemently; and the whole affair already assumes the aspect rather of an attempt to keep Virginia from seceding than of a settled effort to form a bridge for the return of the already se-

ceded States. Nor am I at all reassured by his singular
confidence in Mr. Seward, and his mysterious allusions to
the skillful plans which Mr. Seward is maturing for an
adjustment of our difficulties. He obviously has no respect
for Mr. Seward's character, and in fact admitted to me
to-day as much, telling me a story of Mr. Seward's visit
to Richmond, and of a dinner there given him by a gentleman of distinction whose name he mentioned, but it has
escaped me. At this dinner, according to Mr. Seddon, a
number of gentlemen were invited to meet Governor Seward expressly because of their greater or less known
sympathy with what were regarded as his strong views
on the subject of slavery. Among these was Mr. Benjamin
Watkins Leigh, a man conspicuous for the courageous
way in which he maintained the ground that gradual
emancipation was the policy which Virginia ought to
adopt. I noted this name particularly, because, in mentioning it, Mr. Seddon said: "Leigh couldn't come, and it was
well he couldn't, for he was such an old Trojan that, if
Governor Seward had made the avowal before him which
he made before the rest of the company, I believe Leigh
would have been hardly restrained from insulting him on
the spot."

This avowal was in effect as follows: After dinner, in
the general conversation, some one venturing to ask Governor Seward how he could utter officially what the Virginians regarded as such truculent language in regard to
the way in which New York should treat Southern rec-
lamations for runaway slaves, Governor Seward threw
himself back in his chair, burst out laughing violently,
and said: "Is it possible you gentlemen suppose I believe
any such — —nonsense as that? It's all very well, and in
fact it's necessary, to be said officially up there in New

York for the benefit of the voters, but surely we ought to be able to understand each other better over a dinner-table!" Now, it doesn't matter in the least whether Mr. Seward did or did not say just this in Richmond. Something he must have said which makes it possible for such a story to be told and believed of him by men like Mr. Seddon; and it is a serious public misfortune at such a time as this that such stories are told and believed by such men of the man who apparently is to control the first Republican Administration in the face of the greatest difficulties any American Administration has ever been called upon to encounter. From what Mr. Seward tells me, it is plain that he has more weight with Mr. Lincoln than any other public man, or than all other public men put together; and I confess I grow hourly more anxious as to the use that will be made of it.

THE NEW YORK SENATORIAL CONTEST BETWEEN GREELEY AND EVARTS

I had a long conversation this evening with — —, of New York, on the issue of this senatorial election at Albany, which also puzzles me considerably, and is far from throwing any cheerful light on the outlook. He could tell me nothing of Judge Harris, the newly elected Senator, excepting that there is apparently nothing to tell of him beyond a good story of Mr. Thurlow Weed, who, being asked by some member of the Legislature, when Harris began to run up in the balloting, whether he knew Harris personally and thought him safe, replied: "Do I know him personally? I should rather think I do. I invented him!" Mr. — — says there is more truth than poetry in this. He is a warm personal friend of Mr. Evarts, who was generally designated as the successor of Mr. Seward, and he does not hesitate to say that he believes Mr. Evarts was deliberately slaughtered by Mr. Weed at the instigation of Mr. Seward. They are the most incomprehensible people, these New York politicians; one seems never to get at the true inside of the really driving-wheel. In his indignation against Mr. Weed my friend — — was almost fair to Mr. Greeley. He says that Mr. Weed did not hesitate to say in all companies during the contest at Albany that he believed Mr. Greeley wishes to see secession admitted as of the essence of the Constitution, not only because he sympathizes with the Massachusetts abolitionists who proclaim the Union to be a covenant with hell, but because he thinks he might himself be elected President of a strictly Northern Confederacy. In respect to Mr. Evarts he tells me that he has reason to believe Mr. Seward does not wish to be succeeded in the Senate by a man of such signal ability as a debater, who is at the same time so strong with the conservative classes. As the chief of Mr. Lincoln's Administration, Mr. Seward will have to deal with the reëstablishment of the Union by diplomatic concessions and compromises; and, while much of his work must necessarily be done in the dark and through agencies not appreciable by the public at all, he fears lest the whole credit of it should be monopolized with the public by such a skillful and eloquent champion as Mr. Evarts in the Senate. "In other words," said Mr. — —, "he would much prefer a voting Senator from New York to a talking Senator from New York while he is in the Cabinet." On this theory it is, my friend most positively asserts, that Mr. Evarts was "led to the slaughter." Unquestionably, as the ballots show, the Harris movement must have been preconcerted, and, if Harris is the kind of man my friend Mr. — — makes him out to be, Mr. Seward will have nobody to interfere between him and the public recognition of whatever he may have it in his mind to do or to attempt. Whether a strong man in the Senate would not have been of more use to the country than a "voting Senator" under the present and prospective circumstances of the case, it is of little consequence now to inquire.

Hayne I am told is going home to-morrow, and this Sumter business gets no better. It is beginning to be clear to me that the President means to leave it, if he can, as a stumbling-block at the threshold of the new Administration. And, in the atmosphere of duplicity and self-seeking which seems to be closing in upon us from every side, I do not feel at all sure that these South Carolinians are not playing into his hands. If they could drive away the Star of the West, there is nothing to prevent their driving out Major Anderson, I should suppose.

MR. LINCOLN'S RELATIONS TO MR. SEWARD

New York, February 20th. A most depressing day. Mr. Barney came to see me this morning at the hotel, from breakfasting with Mr. Lincoln at Mr. Grinnell's, to see if I could fix a time for meeting Mr. Lincoln during the day or evening. I explained to him why I had come to New York, and showed him what I thought best of Mr. Rives's letter from Washington of last Sunday. He was a little startled, but insisted that he had very different information which he relied upon, and, finding I could not be sure of any particular hour before dinner, he went pretty fully with me into the question about Mr. Welles, and gave me what struck me as his over-discouraging ideas about Mr. Seward. He assured me in the most positive terms that Mr. Lincoln has never written one line to Mr. Seward since his first letter from Springfield inviting Seward to take the Department of State. This is certainly quite inconsistent with what I have understood from Mr. Draper, and still more with the very explicit declarations made to me by Reverdy Johnson; nor can I at all comprehend Mr. Johnson's views in regard to the importance of Judge Robertson's mission to the South, if Mr. Barney's statement is correct. Of course, I did not intimate to him that I had any doubts on that head, still less my reasons and grounds for entertaining such doubts; but, after making due allowance for his intense personal dislike and distrust of Mr. Seward, about which I thought he was more than sufficiently explicit in his conversation with me, I can not feel satisfied that he is incorrect. If he is correct, matters are in no comfortable shape. He admitted, though I did not mention to him that I knew anything on that point, that Seward has written repeatedly and very fully to Mr. Lincoln since the election, but he is absolutely positive that Mr. Lincoln has not in any way replied to or even acknowledged these communications. I really do not see how he can possibly be mistaken about this, and, if he is not, I am not only at a loss to reconcile Mr. Seward's statements with what I should wish to think of him, but much more concerned as to the consequences of all this. . . .

Mr. Barney said that Mr. Lincoln asked after me particularly this morning, and was good enough to say that he recollected meeting me in 1848, which may have been the case; but I certainly recall none of the circumstances, and can not place him, even with the help of all the pictures I have seen of such an extraordinary-looking mortal, as I confess I ought to be ashamed of myself once to have seen face to face, and to have then forgotten. Mr. Barney says the breakfast was a failure, nobody at his ease, and Mr. Lincoln least of all, and Mr. Weed, in particular, very vexatious. Mr. Aspinwall, who came in just as Mr. Barney went out, confirms this. He says that Mr. Lincoln made a bad impression, and he seemed more provoked than I thought necessary or reasonable at a remark which Mr. Lincoln made to him on somebody's saying, not in very good taste, to Mr. Lincoln, that he would not meet so many millionaires together at any other table in New York. "Oh, indeed, is that so? Well, that's quite right. I'm a millionaire myself. I got a minority of a million in the votes last November." Perhaps this was rather a light and frivolous thing for the President-elect to say in such a company, or even to one of the number; but, after all, it shows that he appreciates the real difficulties of the position, and is thinking of the people more than of the "millionaires," and I hope more than of the politicians. I tried to make Mr. Aspinwall see this as I did, but he is too much depressed by the mercantile situation, and was too much annoyed by Mr. Lincoln's evident failure to show any adequate sense of the gravity of the position.

THE BUSINESS ASPECT OF SECESSION

He had hardly gone, when in came S— —, with a face as long as his legs, to show me a note from Senator Benjamin, to whom he had written inquiring as to the effect, if any, which the farce at Montgomery would be likely to have upon patent rights. Benjamin writes that of course he can only speak by inference, and under reserve, but that, in his present judgment, every patent right granted by the United States will need to be validated by the Government of the Confederate States before it can be held to be of

49

binding force within the territory of the new republic.
No wonder S— — is disquieted! If the thing only lasts six
months or a year, as it easily may unless great and I must
say at present not-to-be-looked-for political judgment is
shown in dealing with it, what confusion and distress will
thus be created throughout our manufacturing regions! I
have no doubt myself, though I could not get Mr. Draper
to see it as I do to-day, that these Confederate contrivers
will at once set negotiations afoot in England and in
France for free-trade agreements in some such form as
will inevitably hamper us badly in readjusting matters
for the national tariff, even after we effect a basis of political accommodation with them. . . .

MR. LINCOLN ON NEW YORK, MAYOR WOOD, AND DEMOCRATIC SUPPORT

My conversation with Mr. Lincoln was brief and hurried,
but not entirely unsatisfactory—indeed, on the main point
quite the reverse. He is entirely clear and sensible on the
vital importance of holding the Democrats close to the
Administration on the naked Union issue. "They are,"
he said to me, "just where we Whigs were in '48 about
the Mexican war. We had to take the Locofoco preamble
when Taylor wanted help, or else vote against helping
Taylor; and the Democrats must vote to hold the Union
now, without bothering whether we or the Southern men
got things where they are, and we must make it easy for
them to do this, because we can't live through the case
without them," which is certainly the simple truth. He
reminded me of our meeting at Washington, but I really
couldn't recall the circumstances with any degree of clear-
ness. He is not a great man certainly, and, but for something almost woman-like in the look of his eyes, I should

50

say the most ill-favored son of Adam I ever saw; but he is crafty and sensible, and owned to me that he was more troubled by the outlook than he thought it discreet to show. He asked me a number of questions about New York, from which I gathered for myself that he is not so much in the hands of Mr. Seward as I had been led to think, and I incline to believe that Mr. Barney is nearer the truth than I liked this morning to think. He was amusing about Mayor Wood and his speech, and seems to have a singularly correct notion of that worthy. He asked me what I had heard of the project said to be brewing here for detaching New York City not only from the Union but from the State of New York as well, and making it a kind of free city like Hamburg. I told him I had only heard of such visionary plans, and that the only importance I attributed to them was, that they illustrated the necessity of getting our commercial affairs back into a healthy condition as early as possible. "That is true," he replied; "and nobody feels it more than I do. And as to the free city business—well, I reckon it will be some time before the front door sets up housekeeping on its own account," which struck me as a quaint and rather forcible way of putting the case.

I made an appointment for Washington, where he will be at Willard's within a few days, and agreed to write to — —. My cousin V— — came to me with a most amusing account of the President-elect at the opera in Mr. C— —'s box, wearing a pair of huge *black* kid gloves, which attracted the attention of the whole house, hanging as they did over the red velvet box-front. V— — was in the box opposite, where some one, pointing out the strange, dark-looking giant opposite as the new President, a lady first told a story of Major Magruder of the army, a Southern man, who took off his hat when a procession of Wide-awakes passed his Broadway hotel last year and said, "I salute the pall-bearers of the Constitution"; and then rather cleverly added, "I think we ought to send some flowers over the way to the undertaker of the Union."

During one of the *entr'actes*, V— — went down into what they call the "directors' room" of the Academy, where shortly after appeared Mr. C— — with Mr. Lincoln, and a troop of gentlemen all eager to be presented to the new President. V— — said Mr. Lincoln looked terribly bored, and sat on the sofa at the end of the room with his hat pushed back on his head, the most deplorable figure that can be imagined, putting his hand out to be shaken in a queer, mechanical way. I am afraid V— — has a streak of his sarcastic grandmamma's temper in him.

THE IGNOMINIOUS NIGHT-RIDE FROM HARRISBURG

Washington, February 24th. Since I sat and listened to the silvery but truly satanic speech of Senator Benjamin, on his taking leave of the Senate three weeks ago, nothing has affected me so painfully as this most unfortunate night-trip of Mr. Lincoln's from Harrisburg here. It is in every imaginable way a most distressing and ill-advised thing, and I can scarcely trust myself to think of it, even here alone in my room. Mr. Seward feels about it as I do, though he affects, with his usual and rather exasperating assumption of levity, to laugh it off. But it has shaken my confidence, and it will shake the confidence of a good many more people in the reality of his influence over this strange new man from the West. It gives a weight and importance of the most dangerous sort, too, to the stories which the opponents of a peaceful and satisfactory adjustment have

52

been so sedulously putting about in regard to the disposition of the border States, and particularly of Maryland; and it can not fail to excite a most mischievous feeling of contempt for the personal character of Mr. Lincoln himself throughout the country, especially at the South, where it is most important that people should at this moment have been made to understand that the new Administration comes into power in the ordinary legitimate way, and will be presided over by a man of law and order, who has confidence in himself, in the people of the country, and in the innate loyalty of Americans to the law. I do not believe one word of the cock-and-bull story of the Italian assassins, which Mr. Seward told me to-day had been communicated to Mr. Lincoln as coming from General Scott; and it was clear to me that Mr. Seward himself did not believe one word of it. Even with the brief glimpse I got in New York of Mr. Lincoln, I am slow to believe in his being so weak and vulgar a man as this performance indicates, and I am satisfied that some extraordinary pressure must have been exerted upon him to make him do a thing which, at any time, would have been deplorable and scandalous, and which appears to me, happening at this moment, to be nothing less than calamitous. I can think of nothing else. It really throws the whole machinery of our system off its center. Are we really drifting into the wake of Spanish America? This can not be; and yet, when we have reached a point at which an elected President of the United States consents to be smuggled through by night to the capital of the country, lest he should be murdered in one of the chief cities of the Union, who can blame the rest of the world for believing that we are a failure, or quarrel with desperadoes, like Wigfall, for taking it for granted? It is sickening.

53

Washington, February 25th. A visit this morning from
Senator Douglas, and who is as much concerned as I am
at the turn affairs are taking. He feels exactly as I do
over this wretched smuggling business; and both startles
and shocks me by what he tells me of Mr. Seward's share
in it, asserting positively, as of his own knowledge, that,
at the urgent request of General Scott, Mr. Seward sent
his son to Mr. Lincoln at Philadelphia, to impress upon
him and his friends the imminent peril they would be in
at Baltimore. I expressed my utter surprise, and asked
him if he had spoken with Mr. Seward on the subject
since Saturday. He had not. "But you must remember,"
he said, "that in all this business General Scott does with
Seward as he pleases; and General Scott is an old woman
in the hands of those born conspirators and makers of
mischief—the Blairs." He went on from this to give me
his reasons for believing that the Blairs were moving
heaven and earth to get control of Mr. Lincoln's Administration; and that they have made more progress that way
than is at all suspected, even by Mr. Seward. I do not like
any of the Blairs, and indeed I know nobody who does.
But of them all I like Montgomery least; and I can imag-
ine nothing less to be desired than his entrance into the
Cabinet, which Senator Douglas regards as inevitable. He
goes further than I can in his views as to the policy which
he thinks the Blairs are bent on cajoling or compelling
Mr. Lincoln to adopt. They are coöperating now for the
moment, he thinks, with the extreme anti-Seward men
both here and in New York. "What they really want,"
said Senator Douglas, "is a civil war. They are determined, first, on seeing slavery abolished by force, and
then on expelling the whole negro race from the conti-

nent. That was old Blair's doctrine, sir, long ago; and that is Montgomery's doctrine, sir," he said, with even more than his usual emphasis; "and, if they can get and keep their grip on Lincoln, this country will never see peace or prosperity again, in your time, or in mine, or in our children's children's time. They will be the evil genius, sir, of the republic. They, and nobody else, you may depend upon it, will be found at the bottom of this abominable smuggling scheme." I asked Senator Douglas how it could have been possible for anybody to persuade Mr. Lincoln into such a suicidal act, unless he is a lamentably weak and pliable character. "No, he is not that, sir," was his reply; "but he is eminently a man of the atmosphere which surrounds him. He has not yet got out of Springfield, sir. He has Springfield people with him. He has his wife with him. He does not know that he is President-elect of the United States, sir. He does not see that the shadow he casts is any bigger now than it was last year. It will not take him long to find it out when he has got established in the White House. But he has not found it out yet. Besides, he knows that he is a minority President, and that breaks him down." Mr. Douglas then went on to give me some painful details as to Mr. Lincoln's domestic life and habitual associations in Illinois, which were very discouraging. He wound up by saying that he had made up his mind to see Mr. Lincoln at once and tell him the truth.

MR. STANTON'S ESTIMATE OF LINCOLN

I called at Willard's Hotel, and left my card for Mr. Lincoln, who had gone out. But, as I was crossing Fourteenth Street, I met the Attorney-General, who stopped me to ask if I had seen the President-elect since he "crept into Washington." It is impossible to be more bitter or malignant than he is; every word was a suppressed and a very ill-suppressed sneer, and it cost me something to keep my temper in talking with him even for a few moments. When he found that I had only met Mr. Lincoln once, to my recollection, he launched out into a downright tirade about him, saying he "had met him at the bar, and found him a low, cunning clown." I could not resist telling him as we parted, that I hoped the President would take an *official* and not a *personal* view of his successor in any relations he might have with him. I think he felt the thrust, for he bowed more civilly than he is apt to do, when he left me. But Mr. Stanton's insolence shows how very mischievous the effect of this wretched blunder has already been; and, while it appalls me even to suppose that Mr. Seward can have had any hand in it, it is not much more satisfactory to believe that he really has so little influence with Mr. Lincoln as would be implied in his not having been consulted as to such a step at such a juncture.

DID FLOYD ORDER ANDERSON TO FORT SUMTER?

Washington, February 26th. At dinner to-day I sat next to Mr. — —, who told me positively, as of his own knowledge, that Anderson's movement to Fort Sumter was made directly in pursuance of a discretion communicated to him as from the President himself, and he added an extraordinary assertion that he knew it to have been recommended by Floyd, and as he believed for the purpose, which of course Floyd was very careful not to betray to Mr. Buchanan, of creating a situation which should make an armed explosion inevitable, and should

56

so force Virginia and the border States into secession. The withdrawal of Secretary Cass, he said to me (and his personal relations at the White House certainly ought to make him an authority, especially when speaking confidentially as he knew he was to-day), roused the President to a sense of the dangerous position in which he is placed by reason of his well-known political and personal good will toward the South and leading Southern men. "He has never been the same man that he was, since that day," said — —. He was positive about the instructions sent to Anderson; and reiterated his assertion two or three times with an emphasis which I thought well to moderate, though, as Mr. Flores, a lively little South American Minister, sat next him on the other hand, there is no great danger, I think, of his having been understood by anybody but myself.

THE CONFUSION OVER MR. LINCOLN'S CABINET

Later on in the evening — — came over and sat by me to urge me to go with him to-morrow to see Mr. Lincoln in regard to the Cabinet appointments. He was much agitated and concerned about them, having gotten into his head, for reasons which he gave me, that Mr. Lincoln, in his despair of harmonizing the Seward men with the Chase men, has concocted or had concocted for him a plan of putting Corwin into the State Department, sending Seward to England, and giving the Treasury to New York. I listened to him patiently, and I own I was startled by some of the facts he told me; but I have pointed out to him that, however close might be the ties between Mr. Corwin and Mr. Lincoln, Mr. Chase could not be counted out in this way unless with his own consent, which I did

57

not believe could be got, and that I am beginning to think that Mr. Chase holds the new President a good deal more tightly in his hand than Mr. Seward does. I declined peremptorily to call upon Mr. Lincoln in the business; though I said I should certainly call upon him as a matter of respect, and that, if he gave me any reason or opportunity to speak of his Cabinet, I should tell him frankly what I thought. I found — — quite as strongly impressed as Mr. Douglas by the machinations of the Blairs, and quite as fearful of their success. He showed me a letter he had received a fortnight ago from Mr. Draper, in New York, expressing great anxiety as to Mr. Seward's position in the Cabinet in case of the nomination of Mr. Chase, and intimating an intention of visiting Washington with several other gentlemen for the purpose of making Mr. Lincoln understand that he must absolutely drop the idea of putting Mr. Chase into the Treasury. I told him that Mr. Weed had to-day expressed the same ideas to me, and I asked him if he did not know that a counter-pressure was putting on Mr. Lincoln to exclude Mr. Seward. "Suppose," I said, "they should both be excluded?"

We were very late, and while the whist was going on I had a very interesting talk with — — about Mr. Benjamin, in the course of which he told me a story so characteristic of all the persons so concerned in it that I must jot it down. We happened to speak of Soulé and the curious letter which he published the other day. "I dined with Benjamin," said — —, "in January, a day or two after that letter appeared, and calling his attention to what seemed to me the nut of it, being the passage in which Soulé eloquently calls upon Louisiana, if she must leave the Union, not to follow the leadership of men who, with

58

the Federal power at their back, had not been able to protect her rights within the Union. I said to him, *'C'est de vous et de Slidell qu'il a voulu parler'?''* Benjamin laughed, as did St. Martin and Hocmelle of the French Legation, who were also of the company, and replied: "Of course" (he was speaking of us), "that is the ruin of poor Soulé, that he can not conceal his morbid hatred of both of us—that, and his congenital incapacity of telling the truth; he loves lying, loves it more than anything else; loves it *jusqu'à la folie!''* Then Benjamin went on to tell a story of an encounter between himself and Soulé, on the way to Mexico, whither Soulé was going to prevent, if possible, the carrying out of the Tehuantepec scheme. When he found Benjamin on board of the boat, which he had not expected, he volunteered the absurd statement to Benjamin that he was only going to Vera Cruz *en route pour Tampico!* Of course he did not go to Tampico, but to the capital; and, when he got to the capital, he opened his batteries on Tehuantepec, by informing the Mexican President that he had been specially deputed by President Buchanan to advise with him on the international relations of the two countries; though he might have ascertained, with tact and a very little trouble, that Mr. Forsyth had already cautioned the Mexican Government, by direction of President Buchanan, against having any dealings with Soulé at all! I did not say to — —, though I was on the point of saying it, that I was not at all sure whether this curious story best illustrated the innate mendacity of Soulé, or the innate duplicity of a more exalted personage. — — is very bitter now against Benjamin, though still under the glamour, as I must confess myself to be in a measure, of his charming personal ways, and his rare and lucid intelligence. At this very dinner to which he referred early in January, — — tells me Benjamin spoke of the arrangements and projects of the Confederate organizers, with an apparent intimate knowledge of them all; saying that the Confederate Congress would assemble at Montgomery before February 15th, and choose a President, so that Lincoln should find himself confronted, when he took the oath in March, by a complete government, extending at least over eight States, and offering peace or war to his choice. — — does not believe the story about Yancey from Montgomery to-day. He thinks Benjamin will be sent as Confederate Commissioner to Europe, to seek recognition; and certainly a more dangerous one could not be selected. He would hurt us abroad as much as Yancey would help us. On reaching home, I found a note from — —, full of hopes for to-morrow, which I can see no reason for sharing, and another from Mr. Weed to the same effect, telling me that Mr. Douglas would see Mr. Lincoln to-night. I do not see that the Peace Conferences have advanced us one step from the point where we were in January, when Mr. Ledyard came to see me, telling me that General Cass had been electrified into better spirits, ill as he then was, by the absolute certainty that Mr. Seward and Mr. Crittenden had so got their heads together as to insure a satisfactory settlement "the very next day." How many days have since gone by with no such result; and what is before us now but imbecility if not worse, in the government we have, and utter distraction in the councils of a government we are to have? Poor General Cass! I bade him good-by yesterday, and I suspect for ever. I should not be surprised if the journey brings him to the end, and I hope he has not been allowed to carry out his purpose of seeking an interview with

Mr. Lincoln. He is not strong enough to bear the excitement, and it can do no good, I fear.

WITH MR. LINCOLN IN WASHINGTON

Washington, February 28th. Half an hour with Mr. Lincoln to-day, which confirms all my worst fears. I should say he is at his wits' ends, if he did not seem to me to be so thoroughly aware of the fact that some other people are in that condition. I told him frankly, on his own provocation to the subject, what I thought would be the advantages of his Administration, and to the country, of putting — — into the Cabinet, and gave him to understand, as plainly as I thought becoming, that he must not look on me as acting in concert with any set of men to urge that nomination, or any other nomination, upon him. I think he saw that I was in earnest; and, at all events, he advised me to write to — — in the terms in which I wished to write to him.

I was sorry to find him anxious about the safety of Washington, and he asked me some questions about Captain Stone, which surprised me a little, and annoyed me more. I told him what I knew of Stone personally, and what had been said to me about him, by the most competent men in the army, at the time when he first came here, by General Scott's wish, to reorganize the militia of the District. He seemed very glad to hear of this, and was very much taken with a story which I told him, and for the accuracy of which I could vouch, that when Captain Stone, upon an urgent recommendation of General Scott, was appointed to the command of the District militia, in January, Governor Floyd was excessively enraged, and tried to get his own nephew, "Charley Jones," who

61

had been previously nominated for the post, and who is a desperate fellow, to insult Stone, pick a quarrel with him, and shoot him. Mr. Lincoln's melancholy countenance lighted up with a twinkle in his eye. "That was not such a bad idea of Floyd's," he said, in a slow, meditative sort of way. "Of course, I'm glad Stone wasn't shot, and that there wasn't any breach of the peace; but—if the custom could be generally introduced, it might lubricate matters in the way of making political appointments!" After a little, he recurred to the dangerous condition of Washington. I then spoke very earnestly, for it was clear to me that he must be still under the pressure of the same evil counsels which had led him into that dreadful business of the night-ride from Harrisburg; and I urged him to put absolute confidence in the assurances of Captain Stone. I told him, what I believe to be perfectly true, that the worst stories about the intended incursions into Washington, and the like, all originate with men like George Saunders, of New York, and Arnold Harris, of Tennessee, once a particular follower of President Buchanan, but now a loud and noisy secessionist—men who came into my mind because I had passed them in the hall of the very hotel in which we were talking, and in which they have been telling wonderful stories of conspiracy and assassination, from the hotel porches, to anybody who will listen to them for weeks past. He listened to me very attentively, and, suddenly stretching out his hand, picked up and handed me a note to look at. I recognized Senator Sumner's handwriting as I took it, and was not, therefore, particularly surprised to find it alarmish and mysterious in tone, bidding Mr. Lincoln, for particular reasons, to be very careful how he went out alone at night.

I saw that Mr. Lincoln watched me while I read the note, and I perhaps may have expressed in my countenance an opinion of the communication which I did not think it civil to put into words, merely reiterating, as I laid it back on the table, my own conviction that there was nothing to fear in Washington, and no occasion for measures likely to influence the public mind unfavorably in other parts of the country. As I arose to go, Mr. Lincoln pulled himself together up out of the rocking-chair, into which he had packed himself, and, scanning me good-naturedly for a moment, said, very abruptly, "You never put backs with Sumner, did you?" I suppose I looked as much surprised as I felt; but I laughed and said that I did not think I ever had done so. "Well, I supposed not," he said; and then, hesitating a moment, went on: "When he was in here I asked him to measure with me, and do you know he made a little speech about it." I tried to look civilly curious, and Mr. Lincoln, with an indescribable glimmer all over his face, continued: "Yes," he said, "he told me he thought 'this was a time for uniting our fronts and not our backs before the enemies of the country,' or something like that. It was very fine. But I reckon the truth was"—and at this point I was compelled against my will to laugh aloud—"I reckon the truth was, he was —afraid to measure!" And with this he looked down with some complacency on his own really indescribable length of limb. "He is a good piece of a man, though—Sumner," he added, half quizzically, half apologetically, "and a good man. I have never had much to do with bishops down where we live; but, do you know, Sumner is just my idea of a bishop." At that moment a door opened, and a lady came in, in not a very ceremonious way, I thought, dressed as if either just about to go into the street, or having just come in. Mr. Lincoln presented me to her as his wife, and I exchanged a few words with her. Perhaps I looked at her through the mist of what Senator Douglas had intimated to me; but certainly she made a disagreeable impression on me. She is not ill-looking, and, though her manners are not those of a well-bred woman of the world, there would be nothing particularly repulsive about them, were it not for the hard, almost coarse tone of her voice, and for something very like cunning in the expression of her face. With the recollection of Mr. Douglas's account of her relations with her husband, the thought involuntarily occurred to me of the contrast between his own beautiful and most graceful wife and this certainly dowdy and to me most unprepossessing little woman. I think if the wives had been voted for, even by the women, Mr. Douglas would be President-elect to-day.

The passages were thronged as I came out. On the stairs I met Mr. Bell, who stepped aside with me for a moment to tell me how much he was impressed with the conservative tone of Mr. Lincoln's mind, and to go over the story I had yesterday heard of the interview of Tuesday night. I did not think it worth while to dampen his feelings by hinting what judgments I had formed of it all from Senator Douglas's account of it, nor to ask him what hope there could be from these propositions of the Peace Congress after what took place yesterday in the New York delegation. But the truth is, I am losing all heart and hope; there has been more Cabinet-making than peace-making in the Peace Congress; and I am beginning to be afraid that the Virginia secessionists are trifling designedly with Mr. Seward and all our friends.

THE RELATIONS OF MR. SEWARD
WITH MR. LINCOLN

Mr. Douglas came to see me late this evening. He has been some time with Mr. Lincoln it seems—last night again, not of course at the jam and "reception," but in a private earnest talk about the Peace Congress and the efforts of the extreme men in Congress to make it abortive. He was more agitated and distressed than I have ever seen him; and it is impossible not to feel that he really and truly loves his country in a way not too common, I fear now, in Washington; but I really can not make out what he expected Mr. Lincoln to do. He told me he had urged Mr. Lincoln to recommend the instant calling of a national convention, upon which point Mr. Seward agrees with him, as his motion in the Senate shows to-day. But he admitted that he had no success in getting Mr. Lincoln to a point on the subject, and this led us to a question of what Mr. Lincoln really means to say in his inaugural. I found that Senator Douglas knew just as well as I knew that Mr. Lincoln has not confided this yet, even to Mr. Seward; but I could not get him to feel as I do how strangely compromising this is to all our hopes of a settlement through the influence of Mr. Seward. How is it possible that Mr. Lincoln can intend to put Mr. Seward at the head of his Administration, if he leaves him thus in the dark as to the purport of the first great act of his official life, now only four days off! I can not even reconcile Mr. Seward's acquiescence in such a course with the respect I would like to feel for him as a man; and it seems to me absolutely discouraging as to the outlook for the country.

Senator Douglas could not or would not see this, even though he admitted that he knew the inaugural address to have been prepared by Mr. Lincoln himself, without consulting anybody, so far as it appears, at Springfield; and though he could give me no good reason for believing that Mr. Lincoln has so much as shown it to Mr. Seward or anybody else since he reached Washington. Everything seems to me to be at sixes and sevens among the very men who ought to be consulting and acting together with united efforts to force the conservative will of the country on all the desperate intriguers of both sections. Senator Douglas tells me to-night that an effort is making now to get, not Corwin, but Sumner, into the State Department, but that Mr. Adams has refused to have anything to do with it. It is only what was to have been expected of a man of Mr. Adams's good sense; it only illustrates the desperation of the rule or ruin faction in the Republican party; and that, I can not help but feeling, is a very formidable force to deal with, especially when brought to bear upon such a man as Mr. Lincoln, with his executive inexperience, and in the presence of the unprecedented difficulties with which he is to deal.

Still I can not think he will let go his hold on Mr. Seward and the great body of strong, sound opinion which Mr. Seward now undoubtedly represents. My chief fear, and as to this Senator Douglas agrees with me, is from Mr. Seward's own friends and representatives here. These New-Yorkers are the most singular combinations of arrogance and timidity in politics I have ever heard or read of. I do not wonder that the Western men dislike them; they are almost as much of a mystery to their nearest neighbors. Before going, Senator Douglas had a word to say about President Buchanan and the South Carolina Commissioners. He tells me that it has now been ascertained that the President nominated his Pennsylvania Collector at Charleston on the very day, almost at the very moment, when he was assuring Colonel Orr, through one of his retainers, that he was disposed to accede to the demands of South Carolina if they were courteously and with proper respect presented to him. They rewrote their letter accordingly, submitted it to the President's agents, who approved it and sent it to the White House. This, Senator Douglas says, was on January 3d, in the morning. The Commissioners spent the afternoon in various places, and dined out early. On coming in, they found their letter to the President awaiting them. It had been returned to them by a messenger from the White House, about three o'clock P.M.; and on the back was an endorsement, not signed by any one, and in a clerkly handwriting, to the effect that the President declined to receive the communication! They ordered their trunks packed at once, and left for home by way of Richmond on the four o'clock morning train, feeling, not unreasonably, that they had been both duped and insulted.

LORD LYONS ON THE SITUATION

Washington, Friday, March 1st. I had a most interesting but gloomy conversation with Lord Lyons this morning, having to call on him in relation to — —'s business with those vexatious people in Barbadoes and Antigua. We fell into conversation after getting through with this; and, though he is the most discreet of men, he pretty

67

plainly intimated to me that he was more concerned as to the outlook than most of our own people here seemed to be. He has old American blood in his veins, which does not perhaps count for much; but his family have had trouble enough with the emancipation business to make him grave, he says, when he contemplates the possible complications of the negro question to arise out of the conflict here, and he put the prospect as to that in quite a new light to me, I am ashamed to say, when he said that, to him, the question of peace or war did not appear to be in the least contingent upon anything that might or might not be said or enacted here in Washington. "How are you going to dispose of the actual occupation, unlawfully, or by force, of United States premises in these seceded States?" he said. "How can the new President acquiesce in that occupation? And, if he does not acquiesce in it, how will he put an end to it?" I really could make no answer to these questions, and they haunt me now as they have not before. How can any negotiations with Virginia affect the situation actually created for us in South Carolina, and Georgia, and Texas, and Florida? Can Mr. Lincoln pass over this difficulty in his inaugural? And yet how can he deal with it as things now stand without bringing the shadow of war over the land? Another thing that Lord Lyons said struck me, which was that, while England could not possibly have anything to gain by a real rupture of the Union, the case was clearly different with France, under her present policy and engagements on this side of the water.

I left the British Minister, feeling as if I had just landed at Washington, and come in contact with the seething peril of the day for the first time. I can not but think that his opinion of the situation is affected by his

European training and ideas, and that he under-estimates the force here of that sober second thought of the people which has saved us so often, and I must hope will save us again now.

INCREASING BUSINESS TROUBLES AND COMPLICATIONS

Washington, March 2d. The distress at home grows hourly worse and worse. And this preposterous tariff which they have assumed to establish at Montgomery points to a still worse state of things. If there are many at Montgomery bent, like some of the worst men we have here, on really driving the two sections into war, they are taking the direct way to their horrible purpose. I can get no positive light as to the actual state of things in regard to Fort Sumter; though — — writes to me from New York that he is positive Mr. Holt has taken measures to secure reënforcements for the fort, and that it will not be evacuated certainly before Mr. Buchanan retires. The news that the Confederates have made Mr. Toombs their Secretary of State is very ominous. There is no wilder or more unsafe man alive; and his last speech in the Senate was as detestable in point of spirit as the maiden speech, on the other side, of that noisy and vulgar cockney Orator Puff, Senator Baker, who came here heralded as such a wonder of eloquence, and who went to pieces so completely in his first effort under the close and withering fire of Benjamin. I met the man again to-day as I passed into the National, and I really could hardly speak to him civilly.

It is such men as he who play into the hands of the worst enemies of the country and of common sense at the South.

There can be no doubt about it any longer. This man from Illinois is not in the hands of Mr. Seward. Heaven grant that he may not be in other hands—not to be thought of with patience! These New York men have done just what they have been saying they would do, and with just the result which I have from the first expected; though I own there are points in the upshot which puzzle me. I can not feel even sure now that Mr. Seward will be nominated at all on Tuesday: and certainly he neither is nor after this can be the real head of the Administration, even if his name is on the list of the Cabinet. Such folly on the part of those who assume to be the especial friends of the one man in whose ability and moderation the conservative people at the North have most confidence; and such folly at this moment might almost indeed make one despair of the republic!

—— has just left me. He was one of the party who called on Mr. Lincoln to-day to bring matters to a head, and prevent the nomination of Chase at all hazards. A nice mess they have made of it! Mr. Lincoln received them civilly enough, and listened to all they had to say. Speaking one after another, they all urged the absolutely essential importance of the presence of Mr. Seward in the Cabinet, to secure for it either the support of the North or any hearing at the South; and they all set forth the downright danger to the cause of the Union of putting into the Cabinet a man like Mr. Chase, identified with and supported by men who did not desire to see the Union maintained on its existing and original basis at all, and who would rather take their chances with a Northern republic, extending itself to Canada, than see the Union of our fathers kept up on the principles of our fathers.

After they had all said their say in this vein, Mr. Lincoln, who had sat watching them one after another, and just dropping in a word here and there, waited a moment, and then asked what they wanted him to do, or to forbear. They all replied that they wished him to forbear from nominating Mr. Chase as a member of his Cabinet, because it would not be possible for Mr. Seward to sit in the same Administration with Mr. Chase. He wouldn't wish it, and his friends and his State would not tolerate it—couldn't tolerate it—it must not be.

Then Mr. Lincoln sat looking very much distressed for a few moments, after which he began speaking in a low voice, like a man quite oppressed and worn down, saying, it was very hard to reconcile conflicting claims and interests; that he only desired to form an Administration that would command the confidence of the country and the party; that he had the deepest respect for Mr. Seward, his services, his genius, and all that sort of thing; that Mr. Chase has great claims also, which no one could contest—perhaps not so great as Mr. Seward; but what the party and country wanted was the hearty coöperation of all good men and of all sections, and so on, and so on, for some time. They all thought he was weakening, and they were sure of it, when after a pause he opened a table-drawer and took out a paper, saying: "I had written out my choice here of Secretaries in the Cabinet after a great deal of pains and trouble; and now you tell me I must break the slate and begin all over!"

He went on then to admit, which still more encouraged them, that he had sometimes feared that it would be as they said it was—that he might be forced to reconsider his matured and he thought judicious conclusions. In view of that possibility, he said he had constructed an alternative list of his Cabinet. He did not like it half as well as the one of his own deliberate preference, in which he would frankly say he had hoped to see Mr. Seward sitting as Secretary of State, and Mr. Chase sitting as Secretary of the Treasury—not half as well; but he could not expect to have things exactly as he liked them; and much more to the same effect, which set the listeners quite agog with suppressed expectations of carrying their great point.

"This being the case, gentlemen," he said, finally, after giving the company time to drink in all he had said —"this being the case, gentlemen, how would it do for us to agree upon a change like this?" Everybody, of course, was all attention. "How would it do to ask Mr. Chase to take the Treasury, and to offer the State Department to Mr. William F. Dayton, of New Jersey?"

— — told me you could have knocked him or any man in the room down with a feather. Not one of them could speak. Mr. Lincoln went on in a moment, expatiating on his thoughtfulness about Mr. Seward. Mr. Dayton, he said, was an old Whig, like himself and like Mr. Seward. He was from New Jersey, which "is next door to New York." He had been the Vice-Presidential candidate with General Fremont, and was a most conservative, able, and sensible man. Mr. Seward could go as Minister to England, where his genius would find great scope in keeping Europe straight as to the troubles here, and so on, and so forth, for twenty minutes.

When he got through, one of the company spoke, and said he thought they had better thank him for his kindness in listening to them, and retire for consultation, which they did. But I fear from the tone and the language of — — that there is more cursing than consultation

72

going on just now. I must own that I heard him with something like consternation. Whether this prefigures an exclusion of Mr. Seward from the Cabinet, who can tell? Nor does that possibility alone make it alarming. It does not prefigure—it proves that the new Administration will be pitched on a dangerous and not on a safe key. It makes what was dark enough before, midnight black. What is to come of it all?

MR. SUMNER AND MR. CAMERON

Washington, March 3d. I received this morning a note from — —, asking me to come at once, if possible, to his house, and going there instantly, as I chanced to be free to do, I found to my surprise that he had sent for me to meet Senator Sumner, whom I found engaged in close conversation with him, and who greeted me with a warmth a little out of proportion, as I thought, to the relations between us, for I have never affected an admiration which I certainly have never felt for Mr. Sumner.

It was soon explained when I found that Senator Sumner had asked — — to send for me in order that he might urge me to call at once upon Mr. Lincoln and represent to him "in the strongest language which you can command—for no language can be too strong"—the dreadful consequences to the influence and success of the new Administration which must follow his nomination of Mr. Simon Cameron to a seat in the Cabinet. Mr. Sumner's conviction was absolute that Mr. Lincoln had bound himself by a political bargain in this case, which would itself suffice to blast his reputation as an honest man were it made known, as it would surely be; but he treated this as a small evil in comparison with the mischief sure to be done by the presence in the Cabinet of such a person as Mr. Cameron, "reeking with the stench of a thousand political bargains worse than this."

When he had abated a little of the vehemence of his language, I took occasion to ask why I should have been requested to intervene in such a matter, and on what grounds Mr. Sumner and — — had reached what seemed to me the extraordinary conclusion that I could be induced to meddle with it. Senator Sumner interrupted me by asking, somewhat more peremptorily than I quite liked, whether I need to be informed of the true nature of this "political Judas from Pennsylvania, whom Providence had marked with the capillary sign of his character, and who might have sat to Leonardo da Vinci for the picture in the Milanese refectory." All this made me but the more indisposed to listen to him, but I finally succeeded in ascertaining that he had sent for me on the strength of — —'s assurances as to the way in which Mr. Lincoln had been kind enough to speak of me to himself. I hastened to assure them both that any good opinion which Mr. Lincoln might have of me must have been based upon my careful abstinence from precisely such interferences—"impertinent interferences," I quietly called them—with his affairs, as the intervention to which they desired to urge me would certainly be. I told them how extremely slight my acquaintance was with the President-elect, to which — — replied that Mr. Lincoln himself had cited my representations in favor of one gentleman whom he hoped to include among his advisers as having been "the most decisive endorsement" with him of that choice. I could only reiterate my surprise; and Mr. Sumner insisting upon his theme, began again with more fervor, if possible. He very soon gave me the true secret of his extreme anxiety on this point. He asked me what interest I or my friends could have in such a preponderance as the Middle States seemed destined to have in the Cabinet if Mr. Seward and Mr. Cameron were to enter it together, and in what way it could advance our wishes or purposes to allow the New England States, "the cradle and the spinal life of the Republican party," to be "humiliated and thrust below the salt at the board which, but for them, would never have been spread"—with much more to the same general effect, but all this with an intensity and bitterness quite indescribable. — — was more temperate in his expressions, but almost equally urgent with me to do what I was compelled again and again in the clearest terms to let them understand that nothing under heaven could make me do, even if I had the fullest belief that my action could in any way affect the matter, which I certainly had not. It astonished me to see how hard it was apparently for Mr. Sumner to understand that my objections to coöperating with — — and himself did not in some way arise out of some relations of my own with Senator Cameron—out of some doubt on my part as to the measure of mischief to be apprehended from Senator Cameron's political reputation, and from the nature of the appointments sure to be made and favored by him.

It was idle for me to assure him again and again that I knew perhaps as much of Pennsylvania politicians in general, and of Senator Cameron in particular, as other people, and should regret as much as he possibly could any "predominance" of Pennsylvania politicians in the new Administration. Nothing could stop him; and he insisted on telling me a succession of stories to illustrate the unscrupulousness of Mr. Cameron, one of which he declared had been told in his own presence and in a company of gentlemen by a chief agent in the transaction, who seemed to regard it, said Mr. Sumner, as a brilliant triumph of political skill, a thing to be proud of, and a decisive proof of the fitness of Senator Cameron for any office in the country.

A CURIOUS CHAPTER IN PENNSYLVANIA POLITICS

It was to the effect that, when Mr. Cameron found his election to the Senate in grave doubt, he turned the day in his own favor by taking a pecuniary risk which eventually resulted in his making a considerable sum of money. According to Mr. Sumner's version of the affair, the person who gave the history of it in his presence, and who is certainly a prominent man in the financial circles of Philadelphia, stated that a leading member of the Legislature (I think he said a State Senator) offered to vote for Mr. Cameron, and to induce two or more of his friends to do the same thing, if he could be relieved of some local indebtedness in the place where he resided and put in the way of a livelihood elsewhere, his constituents being so hostile to Mr. Cameron that it probably would not be agreeable for him to continue among them after Mr. Cameron's election through his help to the Senate. No bribe passed; but the local legislator was appointed to a remunerative position in the way of his calling (as a lawyer, I think) in one of the great Philadelphia corporations, and removed to that city, having previously paid off his local indebtedness with a loan from Mr. Cameron on the security of some stock which he happened to hold in a small railway, at that time of no appreciable value.

The loan was never called for, but through some subsequent legislation the small railway in question was brought into a more extensive railway system, and the collateral in Mr. Cameron's hands advanced to a value far exceeding the amount for which it had been ostensibly hypothecated. After listening to Mr. Sumner for a considerable time, I finally asked him why he did not go himself to Mr. Lincoln and depict the Senator from Pennsylvania in the dark colors in which he had represented him to us. He intimated that he had already done so, and after a little the conversation took a turn which confronted me with the painful conviction that all this indignation about Senator Cameron had its origin not so much in any real horror of the Pennsylvanian element in politics as in the belief, which I hope is well grounded, that the presence of Mr. Cameron and Mr. Seward in the Cabinet will confirm Mr. Lincoln in his disposition to pursue a conservative conciliatory policy which may bring the seceded States back into the Union, rather than a policy aimed at a complete separation of the slaveholding from the non-slaveholding region.

NO WAR FOR THE UNION, AND NO UNION

It did not surprise me, of course, to find Mr. Sumner aiming at such a result, but the acquiescence in his views of — — does both surprise and pain me. I asked them if they did not think it better, from the point of view of the negroes, for whom they seem to be so deeply concerned, that slavery should be held for eventual execution within the Union—now that events had so clearly demonstrated the incompatibility of the institution as a permanent feature of Southern society with that general peace and order which must be as essential to the South as to the North — than that slavery should be excluded from the influences

of freedom in a new confederacy, organized to uphold
and develop it; but I could bring neither of them to reason on the subject. Mr. Sumner grew very warm again.
He was as much horrified as I could be or any man at the
idea of an armed conflict between the sections. "Nothing
could possibly be so horrible or so wicked or so senseless
as a war"; but between a war for the Union which was
not to be thought of, and "a corrupt conspiracy to preserve the Union," he saw, he said, little choice, and he
desired to see the new Administration formed "supremely
in the interests of freedom." As for the slaveholding
States, let them take their curse with them if they were
judicially blinded so to do. He quoted some lines, I think
of Whittier, about their right to make themselves the
scandal and the shame of "God's fair universe," as embodying his conceptions of what we ought now to recognize as the policy of freedom, and then he recurred finally
to the original theme, and once more in concert with — —
began about the visit they wished me to make to Mr. Lincoln. I was forced at last to tell them both explicitly that,
while I fully agreed with them as to the supreme necessity of avoiding any collision or conflict between the
States, and had no fear of any such catastrophe, my hope
of averting it rested mainly upon my hope that Mr. Lincoln was of one mind with Mr. Seward on the subject,
and would direct his efforts to a conciliatory preservation
of the Union; and that neither Mr. Seward nor Mr. Cameron could possibly have less faith than myself in any
"policy of freedom" which contemplated the possibility
of a severed Union, or less disposition to favor such a
policy. It was not at all a pleasant conversation, but it
was a necessary conversation, as I am sorry to find, and
it is painfully evident that the new Administration will

have to contend with a Northern as well as with a Southern current of disaffection and disunion much stronger than I had allowed myself to suspect.

In the evening I saw Mr. Douglas, and, without telling him whom I had seen to bring me to such a conviction, I expressed to him my conviction that unless Mr. Seward entered the Cabinet, and entered it with some colleague upon whom he could reply for support in a conservative policy, Mr. Lincoln would be drifted out to sea, and the country with him.

I found that the incidents of Saturday had been communicated to him, and, as I inferred, though he did not say so, by Mr. Lincoln himself; and I was much relieved to find that he entertains no doubt of Mr. Seward's nomination, and of his confirmation. He told me that Mr. Seward yesterday received assurances to that effect from Senator Hunter, of Virginia, through — —, and he agreed with me that, whatever our private opinions of the political habits and ideas of Mr. Cameron might be, it was most important that no effort should be made to displace him at this hour from the Cabinet, at the risk of seeing a man, either of the type of the Blairs, put in who will press things to a bloody contest, or of the opinion which I fear Mr. Chase represents, that the South and slavery had better be gotten rid of once for all and together. Mr. Douglas used the strongest language as to his own determination to stand by Mr. Lincoln in a temperate, resolute Union policy, and I must own that I never saw him to such good advantage. He was perfectly frank in admitting that he would regard such a policy adopted by Mr. Lincoln as a virtual vindication of his own policy during and before the Presidential election, and that he believed it would eventually destroy, if successful, the organization of the Republican party as a political power; but a man who received a million and a half of votes in a Presidential contest has a right to feel, and Mr. Douglas evidently does feel, that he speaks for a great popular force in the country. But, as I have often felt before, so I felt again this evening, that Mr. Douglas really is a patriotic American in the strong, popular sense of that phrase. He had seen Mr. Lincoln to-day, and he intimated to me that he had heard that part of the message read which touches the assertion of the invalidity of the acts of secession, and that he was entirely satisfied with it. To use his own expression, it will do for all constitutional Democrats to "brace themselves against." I repeated to him what Lord Lyons had said to me the other day, and asked him what ground Mr. Lincoln has taken on the questions raised by the seizure of Southern forts, and by the fortifications put up in Charleston against Fort Sumter. He says that since Mr. Lincoln reached Washington he has inserted in the message a distinct declaration that, while he regards it as in his duty to "hold, occupy, and possess" the property and places belonging to the Government and to collect the duties, he will not attempt to enforce the strict rights of the Government where hostility to the United States is great and universal. I then told him that Mr. Seward, some days ago, had assured me that he believed he would be able to induce Mr. Lincoln to take such a position as this, and that it would suffice, he thought, as a basis of negotiation with the seceded States, and give the people breathing-time to recover their senses at the South; and we came to the conclusion, which I was very glad to reach, that Mr. Seward's counsels must have brought Mr. Lincoln to this stand, in which I have no sort of doubt, and Mr. Douglas has none, that the great majority of the Northern people of both parties will support him.

TELEGRAPHING TO PRESIDENT DAVIS AT MONTGOMERY

It was late when I left Mr. Douglas, but when I reached home I found — — waiting for me with a most anxious face. He opened his business to me at once, which was to ask my advice as to what he should do with a message brought to him by — —, one of Mr. Seward's New York men here, who desired him, in Mr. Seward's name, to have it sent to-night by telegraph to Mr. Davis at Montgomery, Alabama. — — had assured him that it was expected, arrangements having been made that such a message should be sent, and that he would do a public service by sending it. I asked if he had the message, which he produced. It bore a signature not known to me, and was a simple statement to the effect that the tone of Mr. Lincoln's inaugural message would be conciliatory. I asked — — what his objection was to sending such a message, which certainly could do no one any harm and which was probably enough true, when he called my attention to the fact that it was addressed to Mr. Davis as President of the Confederate States. I laughed, and told him that I saw no harm in that any more than in addressing Mr. Davis as Pope of Rome, and that I thought he might safely do as he preferred about it, especially as he had apparently agreed with Mr. Seward's friend to send it. I asked him then why this mysterious friend came to him with such a request, upon which he said that he had known the man very well in Wall Street, and had had occasion to avail himself of his services at various times. I finally advised him to send the message, rather than make any further

81

confidences or communication about it, and to be a little more careful hereafter as to his associates and allies. He was in a curiously perturbed state of mind, and I am afraid has been going into stock speculations again.

As to — —, from whom he got his message, he told me a curious story, which helps to explain the sort of irritation which Mr. Seward's particular followers so often show about him, as well as to confirm my own not very high opinion of some of these New York men in whom he takes such an interest apparently. It appears that, before the message was handed to him, he had a long conversation with — — on the subject of the President's message, and that, after trying in vain to get a definite statement about it from his New York friend, he had twitted the latter until he lost his temper so far as to admit that, when he had pressed Mr. Seward for light as to the President's message this very morning, Mr. Seward had finally put him off with the extraordinary statement that "all he had to do to insure a peaceful settlement of the whole business was to be sure and buy a lot of tickets to the inauguration ball and make it a grand success; that would satisfy the country, and lead to peace."

I really could not stand this, but burst into a fit of laughter, which seemed to annoy — — more than it amused him. He grew quite hot as to Mr. Seward's levity and indifference to the interests of his "friends," protesting that it was nothing less than an outrage on the part of Mr. Seward to put off in this way a man of wealth and influence who was devoted to him, and who had a great material interest at stake in learning whether we were to have war with the seceded States or not, as he was a large owner of steamers which the Government would need to charter if there was to be a war or even a large warlike demonstration. I lost my patience a little with this, and told — — promptly that, if these were the motives of his New York friend, Mr. Seward deserved credit for putting him off with a recommendation to buy ball-tickets, but he came back at me triumphantly with the dispatch to Montgomery which his New York friend had secured at the end of a second visit to Mr. Seward, as a decisive sign of the peaceful prospect before us, and which he finally took away, saying that he would send it.

THE MILITARY INAUGURATION
OF MR. LINCOLN

Washington, March 4th. I am sure we must attribute to the mischievous influence of the Blairs the deplorable display of perfectly unnecessary, and worse than unnecessary, military force which marred the inauguration to-day, and jarred so scandalously upon the tone of the inaugural. Nothing could have been more ill-advised or more ostentatious than the way in which the troops were thrust everywhere upon the public attention, even to the roofs of the houses on Pennsylvania Avenue, on which little squads of sharpshooters were absurdly stationed. I never expected to experience such a sense of mortification and shame in my own country as I felt to-day, in entering the Capitol through hedges of marines armed to the teeth. — —, of Massachusetts, who felt as I did—indeed, I have yet to find a man who did not—recalled to me, as we sat in the Senate-chamber, the story of old Josiah Quincy, the President of Harvard College, who, having occasion to visit the Boston court-house during one of the fugitive-slave excitements in that city, found the way barred by an iron chain. The sentinels on duty recognized him, and stooped to raise the chain, that he might pass in, but the old man indignantly refused, and turned away, declaring that he would never pass into a Massachusetts court-house by the favor of armed men or under a chain. It is really amazing that General Scott should have consented to preside over such a pestilent and foolish parade of force at this time, and I can only attribute his doing so to the agitation in which he is kept by the constant pressure upon him from Virginia, of which I heard only too much to-day from — —, who returned yesterday from Richmond. Fortunately, all passed off well, but it is appalling to think of the mischief which might have been done by a single evil-disposed person to-day. A blank cartridge fired from a window on Pennsylvania Avenue might have disconcerted all our hopes, and thrown the whole country into inextricable confusion.

That nothing of the sort was done, or even so much as attempted, is the most conclusive evidence that could be asked of the groundlessness of the rumors and old women's tales on the strength of which General Scott has been led into this great mistake. Even without this the atmosphere of the day would have been depressing enough. It has been one of our disagreeable, clear, windy, Washington spring days. The arrangements within the Capitol were awkward, and very ill attended to. No one was at his ease. Neither Mr. Buchanan nor Mr. Lincoln appeared to advantage. Poor Chief-Justice Taney could hardly speak plainly, in his uncontrollable agitation.

HOW MR. DOUGLAS STOOD BY THE NEW PRESIDENT

I must, however, except Senator Douglas, whose conduct can not be overpraised. I saw him for a moment in the morning, when he told me that he meant to put himself as prominently forward in the ceremonies as he properly could, and to leave no doubt on any one's mind of his determination to stand by the new Administration in the performance of its first great duty to maintain the Union. I watched him carefully. He made his way not without difficulty—for there was literally no sort of order in the arrangements—to the front of the throng directly beside Mr. Lincoln, when he prepared to read the address. A miserable little rickety table had been provided for the President, on which he could hardly find room for his hat, and Senator Douglas, reaching forward, took it with a smile and held it during the delivery of the address. It was a trifling act, but a symbolical one, and not to be forgotten, and it attracted much attention all around me.

THE BEARING OF MR. LINCOLN HIMSELF

Mr. Lincoln was pale and very nervous, and did not read his address very well, which is not much to be wondered at under all the circumstances. His spectacles troubled him, his position was crowded and uncomfortable, and, in short, nothing had been done which ought to have been done to render the performance of this great duty either dignified in its effect or, physically speaking, easy for the President.

The great crowd in the grounds behaved very well, but manifested little or no enthusiasm, and at one point in the speech Mr. Lincoln was thrown completely off his balance for a moment by a crash not far in front of him among the people, followed by something which for an instant looked like a struggle. I was not undisturbed myself, nor were those who were immediately about me; but it appeared directly that nothing more serious had happened than the fall from a breaking bough of a spectator who had clambered up into one of the trees.

Mr. Lincoln's agitation was remarked, and I have no doubt must have been caused by the impressions which the alarmists have been trying so sedulously to make on his mind, and which the exaggerated preparations of General Scott to-day are but too likely to have deepened.

THE INAUGURAL ADDRESS, AND THE EFFECT OF IT

The address has disappointed every one, I think. There was too much argumentative discussion of the question at issue, as was to have been expected from a man whose whole career has been that of an advocate in his private affairs, and of a candidate in public affairs, and who has had absolutely no experience of an executive kind, but this in the actual state of the country is perhaps an advantage. The more we reason and argue over the situation, the better chance there will be of our emerging from it without a collision.

I listened attentively for the passages about which Mr. Douglas had spoken to me, and I observed that, when he uttered what I suppose to be the language referred to by Mr. Douglas, Mr. Lincoln raised his voice and distinctly emphasized the declaration that he must take, hold, possess, and occupy the property and places belonging to the United States. This was unmistakable, and he paused for a moment after closing the sentence as if to allow it to be fully taken in and comprehended by his audience.

In spite of myself, my conversation with Lord Lyons and his remarks on this point would recur to my mind, and, notwithstanding the encouraging account given me by Mr. Douglas of the spirit and intent of Mr. Lincoln himself, this passage of his speech made an uncomfortable impression upon me, which I find it difficult even now to shake off. There is probably no good reason for this, as no one else with whom I have spoken to-day seems to have been affected by the passage of the speech as I myself was, and I am conscious to-night that I have been in a morbid and uneasy mood during the whole day. Mr. Lincoln was visibly affected at the close of his speech, and threw a tone of strange but genuine pathos into a quaint, queerly constructed but not unpoetical passage with which he concluded it, not calculated to reassure those who, like myself, rely more upon common sense and cool statesmanship than upon sentiment for the safe conduct of public affairs.

Upon the public here generally the speech seems to have produced little effect, but the general impression evidently is that it prefigures a conciliatory and patient policy; and, so far, the day has been a gain for the country. I anticipate little from it at the far South, but much in the border States, and especially in Virginia, which just now undoubtedly holds the key of the situation.

AN INTERESTING MARYLAND VIEW OF THE SITUATION

On my way back from the Capitol, I met — —, of Maryland, who walked with me as far as Willard's. He spoke of the inaugural very contemptuously, and with evident irritation, I thought, and what he said strengthened my own feeling that it will be of use in allaying the excitement which his friends are trying so hard to foment, not only in Virginia, but in his own State. He makes no secret of his own desire to see Maryland and Virginia carry Washington out of the Union with them. When I suggested that other States had spent a good deal of money in Washington, and that there was a good deal of public property here which had been called into existence and value by the United States, and not by Maryland or Virginia, he advanced the singular doctrine that the soil belonging to these States, and that everything put upon it must go to them when they resumed their dominion over the soil. "The public buildings and the navy-yard here," he said, "belong to Virginia and Maryland just as much as the public buildings and the forts at Charleston belong to South Carolina." He did not relish my reply, I thought, which was to the effect that I agreed with him entirely as to the parity of the claims in both cases, and saw no more reason why the property of the United States at Washington should belong to Maryland and Virginia than why the property of the United States at Charleston should belong to South Carolina. He was very bitter about the presence of Senator Douglas at the side of Mr. Lincoln, and generally seemed to think that the day had not been a good one for the disruptionists. I hope he is right, and, in spite of my own forebodings, I think he is. The Blairs were alluded to in our conversation, and he thundered at them as traitors to their own people. He said they were execrated in Maryland, and that no man of them would dare to enter the doors of the Maryland Club, and assured me that, only a few weeks ago, the neighbors of old Mr. Blair had sent him word that "a tree had been picked out for him in the woods." Much as I dislike the Blairs, and dread their influence on the new Administration, I felt constrained to tell — — that, in my judgment, the amiable neighbors of Mr. Blair could do nothing more likely to make his son the next President of the United States than to execute the atrocious threat im-

plied in such a message; and so we parted. This efferves-
cence of local sympathy, in and about Washington, with
the secessionist plans and leaders, is most unfortunate,
for it gives color to the inflammatory representations of
men like Mr. Montgomery Blair, and supplies them with
excuses for persuading General Scott into a course of
military displays and demonstrations, to which his own
unparalleled vanity alone would sufficiently incline him
without such help.

THE CONFEDERATE COMMISSIONERS COMING

On reaching home I found a letter from Mr. Forsyth,
telling me that he will be in Washington shortly, as a
Commissioner from the Confederate States with others,
and intimating his own earnest wish to secure an ami-
cable adjustment of the separation, which he insists upon
as irreparable at least for the present. I shall be very glad
to see him, for he is a man of unusual sense, and I do not
believe he can have persuaded himself into the practica-
bility of the fantastic schemes represented in this wild
confederacy. I hope his colleagues may be as able men as
himself, for, though I do not see how they are to be in any
way officially recognized, their presence here, if they will
hear and talk reason, may be very beneficial just now.

ONE OF THE PRACTICAL CONSEQUENCES
OF SECESSION

Just after dinner I was called out by a card from Mr.
Guthrie, introducing to me a man from his own State,
who wished to see me on "business important, not to himself only." I found him a tall, quiet, intelligent-looking
Kentuckian, who had an interest in a mail-route in the

Southwest and in the Northern connections with it, and who was very anxious to get at some way of saving his interest, by inducing the "Confederate Government" at Montgomery to make terms with him such as the Government had made. The man seemed an honest, worthy fellow, very much in earnest. He had copied out, on a slip of paper, Mr. Lincoln's allusion to his intended purpose of maintaining the mails, and I found that what he wished me to do was, to tell him whether I thought Mr. Seward or Mr. Lincoln would give him a kind of authority to take a contract for carrying the mails for the Government at Montgomery, on the same terms on which he held a contract with the Government here, so that there might be no interruption in the mail service. I assured him that I could not give him any light as to what Mr. Seward or Mr. Lincoln would or would not do, but that I would with pleasure give him a note to Mr. Seward, stating who had sent him to me, and what he wanted. This I did, and he went away expressing much gratitude. The incident struck me as but a beginning and inkling of the infinite vexations, annoyances, and calamities which this senseless and insufferable explosion of political passions and follies is destined to inflict upon the industrious people of this country and of all sections. What is most to be feared is the exasperating effect on the people generally of these things, and my own letters from home bear witness daily to the working of this dangerous leaven among classes not commonly too attentive to political affairs.

THE INAUGURATION BALL

I walked around for half an hour this evening to the inauguration ball, thinking as I went of poor — —'s amaze-

ment and wrath at Mr. Seward's extraordinary proposition that the success of this entertainment would settle
the question in favor of peace. It was a rash assertion on
Mr. Seward's part, for never was there a more pitiable
failure. The military nonsense of the day has doubtless
had something to do with it; for — —, whom I met just
after entering the great tawdry ballroom, assured me that
the town was full of stories about a company of Virginia
horsemen assembled beyond the Long Bridge with intent
to dash into Washington, surround the ballroom, and
carry off the new President a captive by the blaze of the
burning edifice! The place was not half full, and such an
assemblage of strange costumes, male and female, was
never before seen, I am sure, in this city. Very few people of any consideration were there. The President looked
exhausted and uncomfortable, and most ungainly in his
dress, and Mrs. Lincoln, all in blue, with a feather in her
hair, and a highly-flushed face, was anything but an orna-
mental figure in the scene. Mr. Douglas was there, very
civil and attentive to Mrs. Lincoln, with whom, as a matter of politeness, I exchanged a few observations of a
commonplace sort. I had no opportunity of more than
half a dozen words with Mr. Douglas, but I was glad to
find that he was satisfied with the address and with the
general outlook, though he agreed with me that the military part of the business had been shockingly and stup-
idly overdone. He was concerned too, I was surprised to
find, about the nomination of Mr. Seward to-morrow, and
gave me to understand that both the Blairs and Mr. Sumner have been at work to-day against it still. I promised
to see — — in the morning, before the meeting of the Senate, on the subject. — —, of New York, who walked out of
the absurd place with me, and accompanied me part of the

way home, tells me that the real reason of Mr. Seward's anxiety for the success of this entertainment is, that the whole affair is a speculation gotten up by some followers of his in New York, and that he has been personally entreated by a New York politician who is very faithful to him, a Mr. Wakeman, to interest himself in its success!

Certainly Mr. Seward is one of the most perplexing men alive. I can not doubt his personal integrity or his patriotism, but he does certainly contrive to surround himself with the most objectionable people, and to countenance the strangest and the most questionable operations imaginable.

MAJOR ANDERSON AND FORT SUMTER

Washington, March 6th. To-day — — came to see me, having come directly through from Montgomery, stopping only a day in Charleston on the way, where he saw and had a long conversation with Major Anderson, who is a connection by marriage of his wife, and with whom he has long been on terms of particular good will. He astonishes me by his statements, which I can not doubt, as to the real status of things at Fort Sumter. That Major Anderson transferred his garrison to Fort Sumter from Fort Moultrie of his own motion, on discretionary instructions received last winter from the War Department, he has no sort of question; and indeed his very particular account given to me of the circumstances attending the act of transfer is most interesting—so interesting that I have asked him and he has promised to write it out for me, as it is too long for me to set down here. He tells me Major Anderson has no expectation whatever of the reëstablishment of the Government over the seceded States, and that he intends to be governed in his own future course (military considerations and the question of subsistence of course apart) by the course of his own State of Kentucky. He does not sympathize at all with the States which have now seceded, but he thinks the provocation given them in the action and attitude of the Northern abolitionists an adequate provocation; and — — assures me that in his opinion Major Anderson would unhesitatingly obey the orders of a Confederate Secretary of War were Kentucky to withdraw from the Union and join this new and menacing organization. Fortunately, there seems no immediate likelihood of this, but it shows how much more perilous the situation is than I own I had allowed myself to think, and how mischievous in its effects has been the leaving open through all these years of the question of States rights, their exact limitations, and their relations to the Federal Government. — — is convinced that Major Anderson would never have abandoned Fort Moultrie had he not thought wise to remove himself from a position in which he was liable to be commanded by the authorities of South Carolina, his determination being to retain the control of the position primarily in the interest of his own Commonwealth of Kentucky, so that Kentucky might in no way be committed by his action either for or against the retention of the forts in Charleston Harbor. I asked — — to go with me and state these facts to Mr. Lincoln, pointing out to him their grave importance, and the decisive influence which an accurate knowledge of the feelings and disposition of Major Anderson might have upon the President's judgment of what may be expedient to be done in this most dangerous matter. His own conviction as to the quiet and positive character of Major Anderson, of whom he tells

me that, though not a man of unusual abilities in any
way, he is a very resolute and conscientious man, holding
stubbornly to his own ideas of duty, I told him I was sure
would weigh much more with the President than any representations on the subject coming through a third party
possibly could. He was quite averse to doing this at first,
but finally consented, on my urgent representation, to do
so, and I have written a note this afternoon to the President, asking his permission to call on him about a public
matter at some hour which may suit him to-morrow.

THE SECESSIONISTS AT MONTGOMERY

Of the proceedings at Montgomery — — gives me an account at once grotesque and saddening. He tells me that
a sharp division is already showing itself in the councils
of the secession leaders. Mr. Toombs has the wildest ideas
of the immediate recognition by England and France of
the new government, and insists that no concession shall
be made to public opinion in those countries or in the
North on the question of slavery. "Cotton is king" is in
his mouth all the time. Mr. Memminger, the South Carolinian Secretary of the Treasury, — — thinks much the
ablest man they have there, and he takes a more business-
like view of the situation, being of the opinion that, unless something is done to secure the seceded States under
their new nationality a solid basis of credit abroad, they
will not be able to carry on the ordinary operations of a
government for any great length of time. None of them
anticipate hostilities, and I am glad to learn from — —
that the number of persons of any weight and credit
among them, who are disposed so to press matters in any
direction as to make hostilities probable, is very small.

Even in Charleston — — assures me there is a perfect good temper shown in all intercourse between the United States authorities and those who have the present direction of affairs there. At Montgomery — — found the women much more violent and disposed to mischief than the men, many ladies almost openly expressing their wish to see the "Confederate flag" planted at Washington. It appears too, that of this same Confederate flag a number of models have been furnished by ladies. Copies of some of these — — had brought on, and he exhibited them to me. Nothing can be imagined more childish and grotesque than most of them were. The abler men at Montgomery he tells me are urgent that the seceded States should claim the flag of the United States as their own, a proposition which I should suppose would be quite agreeable to Mr. Sumner and others who have not yet got over their disposition to denounce the Union as a "covenant with death and an agreement with hell." I asked — — what these people really mean to do or to attempt to do about patents, showing him some of my letters from home, which clearly indicate the trouble brewing in our part of the country on that very important subject. He could give me no reassuring views of the matter, but, on the contrary, led me to think that the seceded States will try to raise a revenue by exacting heavy sums of patentees for a recognition of their rights within the territory of those States. Such measures, like the adoption last week by their Congress of an act throwing open the coasting-trade of all the seceded States to the flags of all nations on equal terms, are too clearly aimed at the material interests and prosperity of the country not to arouse extreme and legitimate irritation. They are a sort of legislative war against the rest of the Union, which may lead, before

we are well aware of it, into reprisals and warfare of a
more sanguinary kind.

MR. SEWARD'S NEGOTIATIONS WITH VIRGINIA

I asked — — what information he brought as to the relations between the people at Montgomery and the border
States, especially Virginia. He had no doubt, from what
he heard there, that Virginia will secede, and was apparently very much surprised when I gave him my reasons
for believing that nothing of the sort was to be expected.
When I told him, as, in view of his position relatively to
the well-disposed people of the South and of his intention
to see the President to-morrow, I thought it right to tell
him, that a messenger—and a messenger enjoying the direct personal confidence of Mr. Seward—left Washington
this morning for Richmond with positive assurances as to
the intention of the new Administration that no attempt
should be made either to reënforce or to hold Fort Sumter, he was greatly surprised, but was forced to admit
that such a communication might greatly alter the aspect
of things and strengthen the hands of the Union men in
Virginia. He thought it would, if made known, produce
a great effect even at Montgomery.

AN INTERVIEW WITH MR. LINCOLN

March 7th. Early this morning I received a message
from the President, making an appointment for this
afternoon. I called for — — at his hotel and we drove to
the White House. I could not help observing the disor-
derly appearance of the place, and the slovenly way in
which the service was done. We were kept waiting but a

few moments, however, and found Mr. Lincoln quite alone. He received us very kindly, but I was struck and pained by the haggard, worn look of his face, which scarcely left it during the whole time of our visit. I told the President, in a few words, why we had asked for this interview, and — — then fully explained to him, as he had to me yesterday, the situation at Fort Sumter. It seemed to me that the information did not take the President entirely by surprise, though he asked — — two or three times over whether he was quite sure about Major Anderson's ideas as to his duty, in case of any action by Kentucky; and, when — — had repeated to him exactly what he had told me as to the language used to himself by Major Anderson, Mr. Lincoln sat quite silent for a little while in a sort of brooding way, and then, looking up, suddenly said: "Well, you say Major Anderson is a good man, and I have no doubt he is; but if he is right it will be a bad job for me if Kentucky secedes. When he goes out of Fort Sumter, I shall have to go out of the White House." We could not resist a laugh at this quaint way of putting the case, but the gloomy, care-worn look settled back very soon on the President's face, and he said little more except to ask — — some questions about Montgomery, not I thought of a very relevant or important kind, and we soon took our leave. He walked into the corridor with us; and, as he bade us goodby, and thanked — — for what he had told him, he again brightened up for a moment and asked him in an abrupt kind of way, laying his hand as he spoke with a queer but not uncivil familiarity on his shoulder, "You haven't such a thing as a postmaster in your pocket, have you?" — — stared at him in astonishment, and I thought a little in alarm, as if he suspected a sudden attack of insanity, when Mr. Lincoln went on:

97

"You see it seems to me kind of unnatural that you shouldn't have at least a postmaster in your pocket. Everybody I've seen for days past has had foreign ministers, and collectors, and all kinds, and I thought you couldn't have got in here without having at least a postmaster get into your pocket!" We assured him he need have no concern on that point, and left the house, both of us, I think, feeling, as I certainly felt, more anxious and disturbed than when we entered it. Not one word had Mr. Lincoln said to throw any real light either on his own views of the situation or on the effect of — —'s communication upon those views. But it was plain that he is deeply disturbed and puzzled by the problem of this wretched fort, to which circumstances are giving an importance so entirely disproportionate to its real significance, either political or military.

THE INVASION OF THE OFFICE-SEEKERS

We sent away the carriage and walked home. — — called my attention as we passed along to the strange and uncouth appearance of a great proportion of the people whom we encountered on our way or passed lounging about the steps of the Treasury Department and the lobbies of the hotels. I had not noticed it before, but certainly in all my long experience of Washington I have never seen such a swarm of uncouth beings. The clamor for offices is already quite extraordinary, and these poor people undoubtedly belong to the horde which has pressed in here to seek places under the new Administration, which neither has nor can hope to have places enough to satisfy one twentieth part of the number. After dinner I went in to see Mr. Seward, determined, if possible, to get some satisfactory statement as to the outlook of the immediate future from his point of view, and anxious also to ascertain what he knows, if he knows anything, either to confirm or to contradict the story of — — as to Major Anderson and Fort Sumter.

MR. SEWARD'S EXPECTATIONS
OF A SETTLEMENT

I found Mr. Seward in a lively, almost in a boisterous mood, but I soon induced him to take a more quiet and reasonable tone. I told him what — — had told me of Major Anderson, and that I had taken — — to see Mr. Lincoln. At this his countenance lighted up and he exclaimed, "I am so glad you did!" He then went on to assure me in the most positive and earnest terms that he had no doubt whatever that Fort Sumter would be evacuated at a very early day, that there were no military reasons whatever for keeping it, and no more or better reasons for holding it than there had been for holding Fort Brown, which certainly would not be and could not be held. He spoke very severely of what he called Major Anderson's folly in going into Fort Sumter at all—a folly the secret of which, as he said, I had now explained to him, but which was only the greater folly by reason of the motives which led to it, assuming the story of — — to be true, as he added with a great deal of emphasis, "As I have no sort of doubt it is." I asked him how the surrender of Fort Sumter could be effected otherwise than by violence if — —'s story was true, since Major Anderson certainly would not give up the place on an express order from Washington if he cherished the notion of waiting for the action of his own State of Kentucky. That, he replied evasively, would be a matter for the negotiators,

99

and he then gave me to understand that negotiations were, in fact, at this moment going on, which, in his judgment, would very soon relieve the Government of all anxiety on the score of Charleston Harbor and its forts. I then told him what account — — had brought of the state of things at Montgomery, about which, however, he seemed to be himself very fully informed. He could give me no good reason for supposing it, but he seemed to be quite convinced that, as soon as the States of Virginia, Kentucky, and Missouri rejected the appeals of the secessionists, as he has positive information they will reject them, the disintegration of the new-born Confederacy will begin. I asked him how, admitting these expectations to be well founded, we were, in the interval during the process, to get on with our postal and business relations, mentioning to him what — — had told me, that Mr. Toombs and others were strongly in favor of establishing a passport system by sea and land against all citizens of the United States. This apparently made little or no impression upon him, and I must say that I have come home quite discouraged and depressed. In the Senate no one of the Republicans seems to be just now thinking seriously of anything but the new appointments. I have been besieged for a week past with letters and applications asking me every day to see a score of persons whom I hardly know, in order to oblige a score of other persons whom, in many cases, I know only too well. It is a shameful and humiliating state of things, none the more tolerable that it was to have been expected. Mr. Seward was very anxious to get my views as to the proper treatment of Mr. Forsyth and the other commissioners. He seemed inclined to think that a mode might be found of receiving them and negotiating with them, without in any way committing the Government to a recognition of the Government which they assume to represent.

I found it difficult, indeed I may say impossible, to make him admit the hopelessness of looking for such a thing, but I told him frankly that I saw no earthly reason why he should not informally and in a private way obtain from these gentlemen—all of them, as we knew, honorable and very intelligent men—some practical light on the way out of all this gathering perplexity, if indeed they have any such practical light to give. He then gave me to understand that this was exactly what he had done and meant to do, and he repeated his conviction that the evacuation of Fort Sumter would clear the way for a practical understanding out of which an immediate tranquillization of the country must come, and in the not distant future a return of all the seceding States to their allegiance. I can only hope he is right.

THE PROGRESS OF EVENTS AT RICHMOND

Washington, March 9th. — — came in to breakfast with me, having just returned from Richmond. He confirmed the story that an agent has been sent thither by Mr. Seward, with a most positive assurance that on no account shall Fort Sumter be reënforced, either with men or with supplies. He says this assurance reached Richmond the day after the confirmation by the Senate of the new Cabinet appointments, and he was told by — — at Richmond, who certainly ought to know the facts in the case, that Senator Hunter agreed to press for the immediate confirmation of Mr. Seward in conformity with the

101

precedents, on the express understanding that such a message should be forthwith dispatched to Richmond. Certainly, but for the attitude of Senator Hunter, and one or two other gentlemen of like views, the Chase and Sumner men in the Senate would have pretty surely, I think, given Mr. Seward some trouble before that body. As things are, — — thinks the Union men will control the action of Virginia, and that we shall consequently have no war. Heaven grant it! But in all this I do not see what the Government of the Union is negotiating for, or what we are to get for the Union by all these concessions, beyond the boon—priceless, indeed, no doubt—of a peace which has not yet been seriously disturbed, and which the seceded States have at least as great an interest as we ourselves in seeing preserved. The whole thing seems to me much too onesided a piece of business, and I told — — so plumply. Mr. Seward stopped to see me a moment, not long after breakfast, to say, with some appearance of fear, that the President's friends were "pestering" him about sending Mr. Corwin to England, and to intimate that he had put his foot down pretty forcibly in refusing to do anything of the kind. He showed me a note from a common friend of his and of Mr. Forsyth, asking him to receive and give audience to a certain Colonel — —, who had a matter to lay before him of great national importance, and asked me if I would object to seeing Colonel — — myself, as he did not wish to do so, and yet was anxious to ascertain what Colonel — — might have to say. I expressed some perplexity as to how such a thing could be arranged, but he laughed, and said that if I would name an hour there would be no trouble about it at all. I thought this odd, but named an hour for to-morrow morning.

A GLIMPSE OF SENSE FROM THE SOUTH

A letter from — —, at Augusta. She writes in good spirits, but is evidently much impressed with the awkward situation, and with the feverish state of feeling all about her in Georgia. Certainly there is nothing bellicose or savage in her mood, but she tells me that her husband is disturbed and disquieted by what he thinks the imminent peril of great business disasters at the South, and especially in Georgia. He may well feel in this way, with the investments which he has made in factories sure to be ruined by the policy of his "Confederated" brethren at Montgomery.

CERTAIN PLANS OF SOUTHERN LEADERS

March 10th. While Mr. Douglas was talking with me this morning on some propositions which he means to offer in the Senate in a day or two, Mr. Seward's Colonel — — sent his name in to me. I wished to excuse myself, but Mr. Douglas insisted I should not do so, and went away, promising to come back in the evening. I found Colonel — — a very keen, bright, intelligent person, who was full of a great scheme in which he said that Mr. Davis and Mr. Forsyth both were very deeply interested, and in which he believed the eventual solution of the whole trouble in this country would be found. This was neither more nor less than a plan for the building of a great railway to the Pacific through the southwestern portions of the country, on the surveys made under the direction of Mr. Davis while he was Secretary of War. This, he said, the Confederate States Government would at once undertake. It would unite the Confederacy with California, and make it the interest of the whole North to seek a reunion on proper terms at the earliest possible moment with the Confederate States, which would then stretch from the Atlantic to the Pacific, "enveloping Mexico and the Gulf." I listened to the man in silent amazement for some time, for certainly I never heard such wild and fantastic propositions advanced with so much seriousness and apparent good faith, and, finally interrupting him, ventured to ask him what he wished or expected me to do in the premises, and why he should have been referred to me. He seemed not at all embarrassed, but said quietly that he had wished to see me as being a conservative man and a lover of peace, in order to show me that all we needed at the North was to have a little patience, and we should see the way opened out of all our difficulties by this notable project. Is it possible there can be truth in the old notion that, in times of great national trial and excitement, so many men do go mad, so to speak, in a quiet and private way, that madness becomes a sort of epidemic?

Washington, March 11th. The debate on the expulsion of Wigfall has gone off to-day into abstractions, which vex and irritate one in the presence of the practical questions now pressing upon us. I could scarcely listen with patience to Mr. Foster's discussion of the point whether a Senator of the United States ought or ought not to consider his seat vacated upon the passage of an ordinance of secession by his State. Nothing will come of it all, and it only gives occasion to men like Mr. Mason to add fuel to the flame all over the country, by discussing and debating the circumstances in which it will be necessary for them to swell the list of seceders and for their States to go out of the Union.

As for Wigfall himself, his bearing for the last day or

104

two has been rather better than it was on the day of his collision with Mr. Douglas, when he really looked like a tiger, and acted not unlike one. He and all the extreme men seem to be a great deal depressed, I am glad to say, by the intelligence which has crept out of the general agreement of the Cabinet to adopt the course recommended by General Scott on plain military grounds, and order Major Anderson to abandon Fort Sumter.

THE ORDER TO EVACUATE FORT SUMTER

I had a long conversation on the subject with Senator Douglas to-day. He is entirely of my mind that the fort ought to have been abandoned already, and that much valuable prestige has been lost by the new Administration, which might have been secured had orders been sent at once to Major Anderson to that effect. The delay is attributable, no doubt, in part to the dilatoriness of Mr. Cameron in taking up the reins of the War Department; but I am sure Mr. Douglas is right when he lays a part of the responsibility on the influence of the Blairs, who keep pressing for a war policy. Even from their point of view, nothing can be more childish than to make an issue on the holding of Fort Sumter, which has already been abandoned in regard to Fort Brown, and to make that issue on the holding of an entirely untenable place. Mr. Douglas tells me, too, that a further difficulty has been raised by the friends of Major Anderson here from Kentucky, who insist that he shall not be ordered to leave Fort Sumter unless the order is accompanied by a promotion to one of the vacant brigadierships in the army, certainly under the circumstances a most scandalous and even foolish demand to make.

THE PRESIDENT WISHES THE FORT EVACUATED

Mr. Lincoln has assured Mr. Douglas positively, he tells me, that he means the fort shall be evacuated as soon as possible, and that all his Cabinet whom he has consulted are of the same mind excepting Mr. Blair, which is precisely what I had expected. Mr. Douglas says that the President sent for him after his speech of Wednesday to assure him that he entirely agreed with all its views, and sympathized with its spirit. All he desired was to get the points of present irritation removed, so that the people might grow cool, and reflect on the general position all over the country, when he felt confident there would be a general demand for a National Convention at which all the existing differences could be radically treated. Meanwhile he did not see why the Executive should attempt to dispossess the seceded States of the forts occupied by them unless Congress insisted that he should, and gave him the means necessary for the work. "I am just as ready," he said to Mr. Douglas, "to reënforce the garrisons at Sumter and Pickens or to withdraw them as I am to see an amendment adopted protecting slavery in the Territories or prohibiting slavery in the Territories. What I want is to get done what the people desire to have done, and the question for me is how to find that out exactly."

Meanwhile, as I suggested to Mr. Douglas, no one is taking any steps that I can see to find out exactly or inexactly what the people desire to have done, and the secessionists are doing a good many things which for one I do not believe the people at all desire to have done.

BREAKING UP THE UNION BY LEGISLATION

I called Mr. Douglas's attention to a letter received by me from Mobile yesterday, in which the opinion is expressed that, if the mission of Mr. Forsyth and his colleagues turns out a failure, the Confederate Congress will certainly adopt a sort of legal non-intercourse bill already in the hands of their Judiciary Committee, dismissing all cases from the courts to which citizens of other than the seceding States are parties. Mr. Douglas agreed with me, of course, that such legislation as this would be equivalent in some degree to a war, so far as its effects alike upon the country and upon individuals are concerned; and he was not less painfully struck by another bill, a copy of which I have just received from Montgomery, prohibiting absolutely the importation of slaves from the United States unless accompanied by their owners, and with an eye to settlement within the Confederate States. The object of this, of course, is to coerce Kentucky and Virginia, and particularly Virginia, into joining the new government. How long will it be possible for us to sit still and see all the conditions of our prosperity and importance thus nibbled at and taken away piecemeal?

It may be true, as Mr. Douglas suggests, that the introduction of such legislation at Montgomery indicates the obstinacy of the Union feeling in the border States, and may so far be taken as a sign rather of hope than of imminent danger. But the spirit and the intent of it all, so far as concerns the rest of the Union, are not the less hostile and mischievous. Certainly such steps can do little to promote the objects had in view by the Southern Commissioners.

THE DIPLOMATIC PERPLEXITIES
OF MR. SEWARD

March 12th. Mr. Seward is much better to-day, and in unusually good spirits even for him; mainly, I think, because he has succeeded in getting Mr. Corwin to agree to take the mission to Mexico instead of the mission to England. He has news from Richmond, and I understood him from Mr. Summers, that the prospect of defeating the secessionists in the Convention brightens all the time, and that Virginia, after disposing finally of the importunities of the Southern States, will take the initiative for a great National Convention. Of this he feels as confident as of the complete overthrow of the schemes of the fire-eaters by the quiet evacuation of Fort Sumter, which can not now be long delayed. He is very much pleased with the tone and bearing of the Southern Commissioners, he says, "as reported to him," and certainly nothing can be more reasonable or pacific than the disposition shown by these gentlemen so far. But I do not see that they offer any practicable solution—and I told Mr. Seward so—of the situation; nor, indeed, do I see why it should be expected they could do so. The difficulties are not difficulties of sentiment, but of fact. Mr. Seward intimates to me pretty clearly that he already finds Mr. Sumner making trouble for him in the Senate, and pressing him disagreeably in his own department.

He is annoyed too, I thought, at having to send Mr. Cassius M. Clay to Spain, and said with a good deal of sagacity that if he must give a mission to Kentucky he thought it a pity to "waste it on a Kentuckian he was sure of already."

MR. SEWARD AND THE CONFEDERATES

He is hopeful of the success of the Convention plan if we can but get the better of our own mischief-makers here, who are much more dangerous to us, he thinks—and I

108

agree with him—than the people at Montgomery. Without precisely saying as much, he gave me very distinctly the impression that the intentions of the Administration to Fort Sumter have been made known at Montgomery, and have there produced a most beneficial effect. When I called his attention to the hostile and mischievous legislation going on there, he reminded me that the direction of the practical action of the seceded States just now rests with the Executive and not with the Legislature at Montgomery, and repeated several times his conviction that no one in the government there desired a collision more than he or I, which indeed I can readily believe.

I thought Mr. Seward seemed a little annoyed at the present attitude of Mr. Douglas; at all events, he showed an evident anxiety to lead me into expressing an opinion, which I positively declined to express, as to the efforts which Mr. Douglas has been persistently making to drive the Republican Senators into showing their hands, and which of course are not made in the interests of the Republican party. But he had nothing to say when I asked him why none of the Administration Senators were willing to speak for the Administration either one way or the other.

THE SILENCE OF THE REPUBLICAN LEADERS

March 15th. The declaration made yesterday in the Senate, that the seats of Davis, Mallory, Clay, Toombs, and Benjamin are vacant, has envenomed matters a good deal, and the debate of to-day will make them worse. It is a pity Mr. Douglas should have lost his temper, but certainly nothing could have been more irritating than Mr. Fessenden. It was perfectly obvious that the two Republicans who did most of the speaking after Mr. Fessenden —Hale and Wilson— knew Mr. Douglas to be really uttering the sentiments and sketching the policy of the President, and were pretty nearly half willing to admit as much and attack the White House, but they had discretion and self-command enough to forbear, so that Mr. Douglas really threw away his time for the moment. When the news of the evacuation of Fort Sumter comes, though, it will be his turn, and we shall then see collisions which will bring out the innermost truth as to the political chart of the new Administration, and which must pretty certainly lead to the complete reorganization of our political parties, if indeed it stops there.

A PAGE OF
POLITICAL CORRESPONDENCE

Unpublished Letters
of Mr. Stanton to Mr. Buchanan

EDITOR'S NOTE

THE EDITOR of the ''North American Review'' hopes that
it is no longer necessary for him to assure his readers
that he takes part neither with the Trojans nor with the
Tyrians in any of the various controversies which have
so far been evoked from time to time by contributors to
these pages. It is only by way, therefore, of what the
lawyers call ''abundant caution,'' that the editor has
thought it well to request his readers to remember this
while reading the interesting extracts from the ''Diary
of a Public Man'' in 1861, which he is now laying before
them; and that he now reminds them of it in connection
with the even more interesting letters of the late Mr.
Stanton to the late President Buchanan, which appear
below.

These letters were handed to the editor for publication
by a distinguished gentleman, who desires that his name
may not for the present be made known, and into whose
possession they came indirectly from a collection of

private papers left by the late President Buchanan. Of their authenticity no more doubt can be entertained than of the importance of the light which they throw upon that twilight period just preceding the outbreak of the civil war, about which so little has ever been definitely and accurately known, and the interest of which grows with every passing day and month and year. As will be seen, these letters of Mr. Stanton bear directly upon the very grave and momentous events treated of in the extracts which we give in the present number from the contemporaneous "Diary of a Public Man." When we remember that Mr. Stanton, at the time when these letters were written, was bitterly opposed to Mr. Seward, and indeed to the whole Administration of Mr. Lincoln, while the diarist, on the contrary, lived in friendly and familiar relations with Mr. Seward, and was evidently more inclined to support than to assail Mr. Lincoln, the corroborative value of the letters to the diary and of the diary to the letters will be evident. Between them they illuminate one of the most trying and important epochs of our own history, and indeed of all modern history, with a clear and novel light. And, while the editor is in duty bound to make the most formal disclaimer possible of any intention or disposition on his part to accept this light as final, he is sure that he will have the approval of all intelligent and candid readers for transmitting it to them exactly as it comes to him, without assuming in any way either to intensify or to mitigate it. It is tolerably certain that, at the time treated of in these letters and in the Diary, neither Mr. Stanton nor the diarist, nor indeed any man, no matter what his opinions or his powers may have been, can have been in possession of all the facts essential to forming a truly just judgment of the

112

men, or a truly wise opinion as to the tendencies of the hour; nor can we flatter ourselves with occupying a better position in regard to either, until we shall have exhausted all possible means of securing all possible information as to both. — EDITOR.

EDWIN M. STANTON

JAMES BUCHANAN

A PAGE OF
POLITICAL CORRESPONDENCE

------◆◆◆------

Washington, March 14, 1861

Dear Sir: Your favor was received last evening. I shall take care of it, so that when required it may be returned. There is no doubt of Sumter being evacuated; report says the order has gone, but that I think is doubtful. You will have noticed the resolution introduced yesterday by Mr. Douglas in the Senate. That looks like a comprehensive platform for relinquishing everything in the seceded States, and even those who sympathize with them. To me it seems like the first steps toward a strictly Northern non-slave-holding confederacy. In the last ten days nothing has occurred here, to my knowledge, but what you will see in the newspapers. There has been no further action in respect to the Supreme Judgeship. It is generally understood that Crittenden will not be nominated. Judge Campbell has reconsidered his resignation, and will not resign immediately. The Court adjourns to-day. I am now writing in the Supreme Courtroom. If the Court ever reassembles there will be considerable change in its organization. Judge Grier went home sick two days ago. Judge McLean is reported to be quite ill. Lincoln will probably (if his Administration continues four years) make a change that will affect the constitutional doctrines of the Court. The pressure for office continues unabated, Every department is overrun, and by the time that all the patronage is distributed the Republican party will be dissolved. I hope that peace and tranquillity, with cessation from your intense labors, will long preserve you in health and happiness.

Yours truly,
Edwin M. Stanton

P. s. The Supreme Court have just decided Mrs. Gaines's case in her favor, four Judges to three. The Chief Justice, Grier, and Catron *dissenting*. They have also decided that the Federal Government *have no power to coerce* the Governor of a State to return a fugitive from justice, although it is his duty to comply with the demand.

Yours,
E. M. S.

Washington, April 3, 1861

Dear Sir: Although a considerable period has elapsed since the date of my last letter to you, nothing has transpired here of interest but what is fully detailed in the newspapers. Mr. Toucey left here last week; Judge Black is still in the city. General Dix made a short visit at the request of the Secretary of the Treasury. Mr. Holt, I think, is still here, but I have not seen him for several days. You of course saw Thompson's answer and Mr. Holt's reply. I have not had any intercourse with any of the present Cabinet, except a few brief interviews with Mr. Bates, the Attorney-General, on business connected with his department. Mr. Lincoln I have not seen. He is said to be very much broken down with the pressure that is upon him in respect to appointments.

The policy of the Administration in respect to the seceding States remains in obscurity. There has been a rumor for the last two or three days that, notwithstanding all that has been said, there will be an effort to reënforce Fort Sumter. But I do not believe a word of it. The special messenger, Colonel Lamon, told me that he was satisfied it could not be done.

The new loan has been bid for at better rates than I anticipated, and I perceive General Dix was one of the largest bidders at the highest rates. The new tariff bill seems to give the Administration great trouble; and luckily it is a measure of their own. The first month of the Administration seems to have furnished an ample vindication of your policy, and to have rendered all occasion of other defense needless. The rumors from Richmond are very threatening; secession is rapidly gaining strength there. Hoping that you are in the enjoyment of good health and happiness,

I remain as ever, yours,

Edwin M. Stanton

p. s. 12 o'clock. The Secretary of the Treasury has determined to reject all the bids for the new loan under $94. . , . He could have obtained the whole amount at ninety-three and a half. Riggs thinks the Secretary has made a great mistake in not taking the whole sum, and that he will not get as good terms at ninety-three and a half in future. There are no bids here taken.

E. M. S.

Washington, April 12, 1861

Dear Sir: We have the war upon us. The telegraphic news of this morning you will have seen before this reaches you. The impression here is held by many—

1. That the effort to reënforce will be a failure.

2. That in less than twenty-four hours from this time Anderson will have surrendered.

3. That in less than thirty days Davis will be in possession of Washington.

Yours truly,

Edwin M. Stanton

His Excellency James Buchanan

Washington, May 11, 1861

Dear Sir: Your letter by Mr. Magraw was received, and I designed to send an answer by him, but he left here without my knowledge. On the 24th of April, the day after the Baltimore riot, and again on blue Tuesday, the day before the arrival of the New York regiments, I wrote to you.

These letters will probably reach you some time, if they have not already arrived; but I regret their miscarriage, as they kept up a regular chain of Washington events from the date of Lincoln's first proclamation after the capture of Sumter, and since that time incidents have passed so rapidly that I can not recall them in their order.

The fling of Mr. F. W. Seward about "negotiations" would merit a retort if there were an independent press, and the state of the times admitted discussion of such matters. The negotiations carried on by Mr. Seward with the Confederate Commissioners through Judge Campbell and Judge Nelson will some day, perhaps, be brought to light, and, if they were as has been represented to me, Mr. Seward and the Lincoln Administration will not be in a position to make sneering observations respecting any negotiations during your Administration. It was in reference to these that Jefferson Davis, in his message, spoke with so much severity. You no doubt observed his allusion to informal negotiations through a person *holding a high station* in the Government of the United States, and which were participated in by other persons holding stations equally high. I have understood that Judge Campbell was the person alluded to, and that Judge Nelson, and perhaps Catron, were the other persons cognizant of Mr. Seward's assurances respecting the evacuation of Fort Sumter. Mr. Holt is still here; Judge Black has been absent some weeks, but returned night before last. Mr. Holt stays at home pretty closely, and I have met him very seldom, though I occasionally hear of his visiting some of the departments. The state of affairs is tolerably well detailed in the public prints. But no description could convey to you the panic that prevailed here for several days after the Baltimore riot, and before communications were reopened. This was increased by reports of the trepidation of Lincoln that were circulated through the streets. Almost every family packed up their effects. Women and children were sent away in great numbers; provisions advanced to famine prices. In a great measure the alarm has passed away, but there is still a deep apprehension that before long the city is doomed to be the scene of battle and carnage. In respect to the military operations going on or contemplated, little is known until the results are announced in the newspapers. General Scott seems to have *carte blanche*.

He is, in fact, the Government, and, if his health continues, vigorous measures are anticipated. For the last few days I have been moving my family, my former residence being made unpleasant by troops and hospitals surrounding me. In the present state of affairs I do not like to leave home, or I would pay you a visit; but no one knows what may happen any day, or how soon communications may be again interrupted. Marching and drilling are going on all day in every street. The troops that have arrived here are in general fine-looking, able-bodied, active men, well equipped, and apparently ready and willing for the service in which they are engaged. Your cordial concurrence in the disposition to maintain the Government and resist aggression gives great satisfaction, and I am pleased to observe a letter from you in the "Intelligencer" of this morning. I beg you to present my compliments to Miss Lane. There are many stories afloat among the ladies in the city that would amuse her, but, as they are no duobt told her by lady correspondents, it is needless for me to repeat them. I hope you may continue in the enjoyment of good health, and remain with sincere regard,

Yours truly,
Edwin M. Stanton

Washington, May 19, 1861

Dear Sir: You will see in the New York papers Judge Campbell's report of the negotiation between himself and Mr. Seward, to which I referred in my letter of last week. They had been related to me by the Judge, about the time they closed. Mr. Seward's silence will not relieve him from the imputation of deceit and double dealing in the minds of many, although I do not believe it can justly be imputed to him. I have no doubt he believed that Sumter would be evacuated, as he stated it would be. But the war-party overruled him with Lincoln, and he was forced to give up, but could not give up his office. That is a sacrifice no Republican will be apt to make. But this correspondence shows that Mr. Frederick Seward was not in the line of truth when he said that negotiations ceased on the 4th of March. The "New York Evening Post" is very severe on Judge Campbell, and very unjustly so, for the Judge has been as anxiously and patriotically earnest to preserve the Government as any man in the United States, and he has sacrificed more than any Southern man rather than yield to the secessionists. I regret the treatment he has received from Mr. Seward and the "Post."

Nothing new has transpired here since my last letter. I am perfectly convinced that an attack will be made and a battle fought for this city before long.

With sincere regard, I remain yours truly,
Edwin M. Stanton

His Excellency James Buchanan

Washington, June 8, 1861

Dear Sir: Your friends here are very much gratified by Judge Black's report of improvement in your health. The accounts we have had occasioned a great deal of solicitude concerning you; but I trust that you may now be speedily restored. I have not written to you for some time, because there was nothing to communicate that would cheer or gratify you. While every patriot has rejoiced at the enthusiastic spirit with which the nation has aroused to maintain its existence and honor, the peculation and fraud that immediately spring up, to prey upon the volunteers and grasp the public money as plunder and spoil, have created a strong feeling of loathing and disgust. And no sooner had the appearance of imminent danger passed away, and the Administration recovered from its panic, than a determination became manifest to give a strict party direction, as far as possible, to the great national movement. After a few Democratic appointments, as Butler and Dix, everything else has been exclusively devoted to black Republican interests. This has already excited a strong reactionary feeling not only in New York, but in the Western States. General Dix informs me that he has been so badly treated by Cameron, and so disgusted by the general course of the Administration, that he intends immediately to resign. This will be followed by a withdrawal of financial confidence and support to a very great extent. Indeed, the course of things for the last four weeks has been such as to excite distrust in every department of the Government. The military movements, or rather inaction, also excite great apprehension. It is believed that Davis and Beauregard are both in this vicinity—one at Harper's Ferry, the other at Manassas Gap—and that they can concentrate over sixty thousand troops. Our whole force does not exceed forty-five thousand. It is also reported that discord exists between the Cabinet and General Scott in respect to important points of strategy.

Our condition, therefore, seems to be one of even greater danger than at any former period, for the consequence of success by the secessionists would be far more extensive and irremediable than if the Capitol had been seized weeks ago. Ould is reported as having gone off and joined the secessionists. Harvey, the new Minister to Spain, it is discovered, was a correspondent with the secessionists, and communicated the designs and operations of the Government to Judge McGrath. It is supposed he will be recalled. Cassius Clay has been playing the fool at London, by writing letters to the "Times," which that paper treats with ridicule and contempt. The impression here is, that the decided and active countenance and support of the British Government will be given to the Southern Confederacy. Mr. Holt is still here, but I seldom see him. Judge Black is also here. I should have visited you, but dare not leave town even for one night. Our troops have slept on their arms nearly every night for a week, anticipating attack.

Hoping to hear of your restoration to good health,

I remain, as ever, truly yours,

Edwin M. Stanton

Washington, June 12, 1861

Dear Sir: I had written to you the day before your letter was received, and am very glad to learn that your health is still improving. Shortly after the 4th of March I saw Mr. Weaver, and told him to let me know, in case there should appear any disposition to interfere with him, and I would exert myself to have him retained. He expressed himself so confidently of his security, that any interposition of mind would have appeared gratuitous, if not impertinent. But, before your last letter reached here, he called and said he had been removed. He said he did not desire to be reinstated in it, preferring to enter the military service, and desiring a captain's commission. While I think his restoration might be accomplished, the other is more doubtful, as it is generally understood that Mr. Cameron has bestowed all the military posts. I shall, however, do all in my power to accomplish what Mr. Weaver desires, on account of the interest you take in his welfare. We have this morning disastrous news from Fortress Monroe. The rumor is that the sacrifice of life at Bethel Bridge was very great, and it is in a great measure attributed to the incompetence of the commanding officer. There is much reason to fear that other disasters from similar cause will occur. The recent appointments in the army are generally spoken of with great disapprobation. General Dix is very much chagrined with the treatment he has received from the War Department, and on Saturday I had a letter declaring his intention to resign immediately. He would in my opinion be a serious loss to the service. The rumored appointment of Cummings of the "Bulletin," as brigadier-general and quartermaster-general, has produced very general dissatisfaction and distrust. The appointment has been announced as having been certainly made, but I do not believe that it has been. I had a letter this week from your friend General Harney. He feels himself very badly treated by the Administration. Last month he was ordered to Washington without any reason but suspicion of his loyalty. Being satisfied on that point, he was restored to his command, and is now again superseded, without any explanation, and is disgraced by being left without any command. Since this letter was commenced, the brother of General Butler has arrived from Fort Monroe, and reports the whole loss of our troops at fourteen killed and forty-four wounded. This is so greatly below the former reports, which set down our loss at over one thousand, that it affords great relief. There is great anxiety to hear from Harper's Ferry. The movement in that direction a few days ago, you have no doubt seen in the papers. Much apprehension is felt here, as to the expedition, and there is some uneasiness lest an attack on this city will be induced by withdrawal of so large a portion of the military force.

Harvey's treachery is much talked of. The foreign indications by yesterday's steamer are considered more favorable than heretofore.

I beg you to present my compliments to Miss Lane, and with sincere regard,

I remain yours truly,
Edwin M. Stanton

Washington, July 16, 1861

Dear Sir: Your favor, with the continuation of the historical sketch, was duly received. Last evening Judge Black and General Dix met at my house and consulted together in regard to it. We concur in opinion that a publication at present would accomplish no good. The public mind is too much excited on other topics to give attention to the past, and it would only afford occasion for fresh, malignant attacks upon you. . . . At all events a stronger impression will hereafter be produced when the public feeling is more tranquil. The narration appears to me to be a clear and accurate statement of the events of the period to which it relates, with one exception of no material consequence, in respect to which, the recollection of Judge Black, General Dix, and myself is somewhat different from the statement. Speaking of the order to the Brooklyn not to disembark the forces sent to Pickens, unless that fort were attacked, you mention it as having been made with the entire unanimity of your Cabinet and the approval of General Scott. That he approved it is fully shown by Mr. Holt's note to you; but our recollection is, that in the Cabinet it was opposed by Judge Black, General Dix, and myself. I do not know that there is now any reason to question the wisdom of the measure. It may have saved Pickens from immediate attack at that time; and I have understood that General Scott says that Pickens could not have been successfully defended if it had then been attacked, and that he speaks of this as a blunder of the Confederates. In this view, the wisdom of the measure is fully vindicated; and at the time it was supported by the Secretary of War and Secretary of the Navy, to whose departments the subject appertained. So far, however, as your Administration is concerned, its policy in reference to both Sumter and Pickens is fully vindicated by the course of the present Administration for forty days after the inauguration of Lincoln. No use was made of the means that had been prepared for reënforcing Sumter. A Republican Senator informed me, a short time ago, that General Scott personally urged him to consent to the evacuation of both Sumter and Pickens; and it is a fact of general notoriety, published in all the papers at the time and never contradicted, that not only the General, but other military men who were consulted, were in favor of that measure. Whatever may be said . . . now, I think that the public will be disposed to do full justice to your efforts to avert the calamity of civil war; and every month for a long time to come will, I am afraid, furnish fresh evidence of the magnitude of that calamity. The impression that Mr. Weaver had received an army appointment proved to be a mistake; it was another Weaver who was appointed.

General Dix is still here. He has been shamefully treated by the Administration. We are expecting a general battle to be commenced at Fairfax to-day, and conflicting opinions of the result are entertained.

With sincere regard, I remain, as ever,

Truly yours,

Edwin M. Stanton

His Excellency James Buchanan

Washington, July 26, 1861

Dear Sir: Three days ago I received the inclosed letters under cover addressed to me. Upon reading the first sentence, I perceived there must be some mistake, and, turning over the leaf, saw that the address was to Judge Black, and I therefore return them unread. I should have handed them to him, but have not seen him since they were received, and am informed that he left here some days ago. The dreadful disaster of Sunday can scarcely be mentioned. The imbecility of this Administration culminated in that catastrophe—an irretrievable misfortune and national disgrace never to be forgotten are to be added to the ruin of all peaceful pursuits and national bankruptcy as the result of Lincoln's "running the machine" for five months. You perceive that Bennett is for a change of the Cabinet, and proposes for one of the new Cabinet Mr. Holt. . . . It is not unlikely that some change in the War and Navy Departments may take place, but none beyond these two departments until Jefferson Davis turns out the whole concern. The capture of Washington seems now to be inevitable—during the whole of Monday and Tuesday it might have been taken without any resistance. The rout, overthrow, and utter demoralization of the whole army is complete. Even now I doubt whether any serious opposition to the entrance of the Confederate forces could be offered. While Lincoln, Scott, and the Cabinet are disputing who is to blame, the city is unguarded and the enemy at hand. General McClellan reached here last evening. But, if he had the ability of Caesar, Alexander, or Napoleon, what can he accomplish? Will not Scott's jealousy, Cabinet intrigues, Republican interference, thwart him at every step? While hoping for the best, I can not shut my eyes against the dangers that beset the Government, and especially this city. It is certain that Davis was in the field on Sunday, and the Secessionists here assert that he headed in person the last victorious charge. General Dix is in Baltimore. After three weeks' neglect and insult he was sent there. The warm debate between Douglas's friend Richardson and Kentucky Burnett has attracted some interest, but has been attended with no bellicose result. Since this note was commenced, the morning paper has come in, and I see that McClellan did *not* arrive last night, as I was informed he had. General Lee was after him, but will have to wait awhile before they can meet.

Yours truly,

Edwin M. Stanton

His Excellency James Buchanan

BIOGRAPHICAL DATA

The opening lines of the first magazine installment of the "Diary" contain an example of the method used throughout by the writer as to the mention or suppression of the names of the men who figure in his records. In his first sentence he refers to "A long conversation . . . with Mr. Orr." In the second sentence he refers to "Mr. B——." In the following list the significance of the names mentioned is briefly indicated, but no guesses are offered for the filling of the blanks. While some of the names are very familiar, it seems best to include all without reference to their relative importance. Figures in brackets indicate the pages in the "Diary" where each person is mentioned.

Charles Francis Adams of Massachusetts resigned from the House of Representatives in 1861 to become Minister to England. [66]

Major Robert Anderson of Kentucky commanded the forts in Charleston Harbor and defended Fort Sumter. [31, 33, 34, 36, 47, 56, 57, 92, 93, 97, 99, 105]

William H. Aspinwall of New York City, a merchant and capitalist, held no office although he was interested in politics and was active in support of Lincoln. [41, 42, 49]

Edward D. Baker, Senator from Oregon, an old Illinois friend of Lincoln, was killed at Ball's Bluff in October, 1861. [69]

Hiram Barney was appointed by Lincoln to one of the greatest patronage offices at his disposal, the Collector of the Port of New York. [47, 48, 49, 51]

John Bell of Tennessee served fourteen years in the House and twelve in the Senate and ran with Edward Everett on the "Constitutional Union" Presidential ticket in 1860. [64]

Judah P. Benjamin of Louisiana, an eminent lawyer, "withdrew" from the Senate on February 4, 1861, and became in succession Attorney General, Secretary of War and Secretary of State in the Confederate Cabinet. [41, 42, 43, 49, 52, 58, 59, 60, 69, 109]

Francis Preston Blair, Sr., of Maryland, had been a Jacksonian Democrat, a Free Soiler and a supporter of Lincoln. [54, 55, 58, 79, 83, 88, 91, 105]

Francis Preston Blair, Jr., of Missouri, was an "unyielding Unionist," a Congressman and Civil War general.

Montgomery Blair of Maryland became Lincoln's Postmaster General. [54, 55, 58, 79, 83, 88, 89, 91, 105, 106]

John C. Breckinridge of Kentucky, Vice-President with Buchanan and defeated Presidential candidate of the Southern wing of the Democratic Party in 1860; elected Senator, he remained a member until "expelled" in December, 1861, after which he served the Confederacy as a soldier and as Davis's last Secretary of War. [34, 39]

James Buchanan, President of the United States, March 4, 1857, to March 4, 1861. [31, 34, 37, 39, 40, 43, 56, 59, 62, 67, 69, 84]

Simon Cameron of Pennsylvania, Senator, Secretary of War and Minister to Russia. [73, 74, 75, 76, 77, 78, 79, 105]

Lewis Cass of Michigan, Senator, Democratic Presidential candidate in 1848, Buchanan's Secretary of State until his resignation on December 12, 1860, in protest against the decision not to reinforce the Charleston forts. [57, 60]

Salmon P. Chase of Ohio, Senator, Governor, Secretary of the Treasury; appointed by Lincoln to the Supreme Court. [57, 58, 70, 71, 72, 79, 102]

Cassius M. Clay of Kentucky, Abolitionist, Minister to Russia until succeeded by Cameron. [108]

Clement Claiborne Clay, Jr., of Alabama, Senator from 1853 until his "withdrawal" on January 21, 1861; the Secretary of the Senate carried the names of Clay and several other Southern Senators on the roll until by Senate resolution of March 14 he was directed to omit them. [109]

Thomas Corwin of Ohio, Governor, Senator, Fillmore's Secretary of the Treasury, sent by Lincoln as Minister to Mexico. [57, 66, 102, 108]

John J. Crittenden of Kentucky, Governor, Fillmore's Attorney General, Senator, Unionist Congressman in 1861. [60]

Caleb Cushing of Massachusetts, Minister to China, Attorney General in the Pierce Cabinet; Buchanan sent him to South Carolina to delay if possible the adoption of an Ordinance of Secession. [38, 40]

Jefferson Davis of Mississippi, Senator, Secretary of War under Pierce, and President of the Confederacy. [81, 103, 109]

William L. Dayton of New Jersey, State Supreme Court Judge, Whig Senator, on the Republican ticket with Fremont in 1856, appointed Minister to France by Lincoln in 1861. [72]

Abner Doubleday of New York, army officer, said to

have aimed the first shot from Sumter in reply to the bombardment. [36]

Stephen A. Douglas of Illinois, Congressman and Senator, the Northern Democrats' candidate for the Presidency in 1860. [36, 37, 39, 43, 54, 55, 58, 60, 64, 65, 66, 67, 79, 80, 81, 84, 85, 86, 88, 91, 103, 105, 106, 107, 109, 110]

Simeon Draper of New York City, merchant, backed by Seward and Weed for Collector of the Port and appointed by Lincoln in 1864 as successor to Barney. [48, 50, 58]

William M. Evarts of New York, lawyer and orator, chairman of the State delegation to the 1860 Chicago Convention, defeated for the Senate in 1861. [45, 46]

William Pitt Fessenden of Maine, Whig Congressman and Senator, a member of the Peace Convention of 1861, followed Chase as Secretary of the Treasury. [109, 110]

Don Fernando Flores, on a mission from Ecuador. [57]

John B. Floyd of Virginia, Buchanan's Secretary of War, a States' Rights Democrat who opposed secession until he retired from the Cabinet, owing to the President's refusal to order Anderson back to Fort Moultrie. [31, 38, 39, 56, 61, 62]

John Forsyth of Alabama, Minister to Mexico, one of three Commissioners who arrived in Washington March 5, 1861, to negotiate friendly relations with the United States. [59, 89, 100, 102, 103, 107]

Lafayette S. Foster of Connecticut, Senator and State Supreme Court Judge. [104]

John Charles Fremont, known as ''The Pathfinder'' for his explorations in the West; Republican candidate for the Presidency in 1856. [72]

132

Horace Greeley of New York, journalist, founder of the *New York Tribune*. [46]

Moses H. Grinnell of New York City, merchant and ship-owner, served one term in Congress, staunch champion of Unionism. [47]

James Guthrie of Kentucky, Secretary of the Treasury under Pierce, member of the 1861 Peace Convention, Unionist Democrat. [89]

John P. Hale of New Hampshire, Congressman and Senator, Free Soil Presidential candidate in 1852. [110]

Arnold Harris "of Tennessee," from 1848 to 1861 commission merchant in New Orleans, conducted for a time the newspaper called *The States* which, he declared, "was not surpassed in the vigor of its attacks on the usurpations of Lincoln by any in the Confederate States." Taken prisoner after Bull Run, Harris was imprisoned in Richmond for six months, in spite of the protests of friends who cited his Southern sympathies. Died in Kentucky in 1866. This identification of the most elusive of all the men named by the Diarist seems correct, although he seems to have come from New York rather than from Tennessee as the Public Man states. Harris was in Washington early in 1861, and Mrs. Chesnut, in her *Diary from Dixie,* alludes to his presence in Richmond late in July. [62]

Ira Harris of New York, State Supreme Court Judge, defeated Evarts for the Senate in the election of February 3, 1861. [45, 46]

Colonel I. W. Hayne of South Carolina, sent to Washington by Governor Pickens "to demand delivery of Fort Sumter to the constituted authorities of the State."[47]

Joseph Holt of Kentucky succeeded Floyd as Secretary of War on January 18, 1861, by transfer from the office of Postmaster General; appointed Judge Advocate General by Lincoln in 1862. [69]

Robert M. T. Hunter of Virginia, Senator who "withdrew" on March 28, 1861; he had been a member of the Senate Committee of Thirteen. [79, 101, 102]

Reverdy Johnson of Maryland, Whig Senator, later a Democrat, Attorney General in Taylor's Cabinet, member of the Peace Convention of 1861, a noted Constitutional lawyer who represented the defense in the Dred Scott case. [48]

Charles Jones, nephew of the Secretary of War in Buchanan's Cabinet. [61]

Henry Ledyard of Michigan, son-in-law of Lewis Cass, and for a time his Assistant Secretary of State. [60]

Benjamin Watkins Leigh of Virginia, Senator, died in 1849. In 1846 Seward visited him bearing a letter from Daniel Webster. [44]

Abraham Lincoln of Illinois, President of the United States, March 4, 1861, to April 15, 1865. [36, 37, 45, 46, 47, 48, 49, 50, 52, 53, 54, 55, 56, 57, 58, 60, 61, 62, 63, 64, 65, 66, 68, 70, 71, 72, 73, 74, 77, 78, 79, 80, 81, 84, 85, 86, 87, 88, 90, 93, 97, 98, 99, 106]

Lord Lyons, British career diplomat, Minister in Washington from 1859 to March, 1865. [67, 80, 86]

Stephen R. Mallory of Florida, Senator from 1851 until his "withdrawal" on January 21, 1861; Confederate Secretary of the Navy. [109]

James M. Mason of Virginia, Senator from 1847 until March 28, 1861; Confederate Commissioner to England and France. [104]

Christopher G. Memminger of South Carolina, "financial statesman," Confederate Secretary of the Treasury. [94]

James L. Orr of South Carolina, Congressman, member of the Secession Convention, one of three Commissioners sent to Washington to treat for the surrender of the forts in Charleston Harbor. [31, 33, 34, 35, 36, 40, 67]

Francis W. Pickens of South Carolina, Congressman, Minister to Russia, Governor. [36]

Josiah Quincy of Massachusetts, Federalist Congressman, Mayor of Boston, President of Harvard College. His startling speech in 1811 was to the effect that to admit Louisiana, a territory outside the original Union, by majority vote and without consent of the original partners, would "virtually dissolve" the Union and justify separation. [32, 83]

William C. Rives of Virginia, Congressman, Minister to France, Senator, member of the 1861 Peace Convention, delegate from Virginia to the Confederate Provisional Congress. [47]

John Robertson of Virginia, commissioned in January, 1861, by the General Assembly to appeal to the seceded states "to abstain from all acts of a hostile tendency until a further effort shall be made to terminate existing differences by an honorable and peaceful adjustment." [48]

George N. Sanders (Saunders) of Kentucky, lobbyist, Navy agent at New York City, Confederate agent in Europe. [62]

Winfield Scott of Virginia, "hero of two wars," Whig candidate for President in 1852, for twenty years commanding general of the United States Army. [53, 54, 61, 84, 86, 89, 105]

James A. Seddon of Virginia, Congressman, member of the 1861 Peace Convention, delegate to the Confederate

Provisional Congress, Confederate Secretary of War. [44, 45]

William H. Seward of New York, Governor, Senator, Secretary of State under Lincoln and Johnson. [33, 34, 37, 41, 44, 45, 46, 47, 48, 51, 52, 53, 54, 56, 57, 58, 60, 64, 65, 66, 70, 71, 72, 73, 75, 77, 78, 79, 80, 81, 82, 83, 90, 91, 92, 96, 98, 99, 100, 101, 102, 103, 107, 108, 109]

John Slidell of Louisiana, Senator, "withdrew" on February 4, 1861, Confederate Commissioner to France. [59]

Pierre Soulé of Louisiana, Senator, Minister to Spain, author of the Ostend Manifesto which was signed also by Buchanan, then Minister at London, and by Mason, then Minister at Paris, outlining what they held to be the duty of the United States to Cuba. Soulé opposed secession but stood with his state. [58, 59]

Edwin M. Stanton of Ohio, Attorney General for a time under Buchanan; succeeded Cameron as Lincoln's Secretary of War. [56]

Charles P. Stone, West Point graduate, with Scott in the Mexican War; resigned, but was mustered into the service as Colonel of the District of Columbia Volunteers in 1861, and soon was reappointed to the regular Army. [61, 62]

George W. Summers of Virginia, circuit judge, delegate to the Secession Convention at Richmond in 1861. [108]

Charles Sumner of Massachusetts, Senator from 1851 until his death in 1874. [62, 63, 66, 73, 74, 75, 76, 77, 78, 91, 95, 102, 108]

Roger B. Taney of Maryland, Attorney General and Secretary of the Treasury for a time under Jackson, Chief Justice of the United States Supreme Court from 1836 to 1864. [84]

Zachary Taylor, President of the United States, March 4, 1849, to July 9, 1850. [50]

Robert Toombs of Georgia, Congressman and Senator, "withdrew" on February 4, 1861; a member of the Confederate Provisional Congress and Secretary of State. [69, 94, 100, 109]

Benjamin F. Wade of Ohio, Senator from 1851 to 1869. [36, 37]

Abram Wakeman of New York, Congressman, appointed postmaster of New York City in 1862, and surveyor of the Port of New York in 1864. [92]

Thurlow Weed of New York, controlled *The Albany Evening Journal* for thirty-five years and wielded great political influence. [45, 46, 49, 58, 60]

Gideon Welles of Connecticut, Lincoln's Secretary of the Navy. [47]

Louis T. Wigfall of Texas, Senator from December, 1859, until his "withdrawal," on March 23, 1861. [38, 39, 53, 104]

Henry Wilson of Massachusetts, Senator from 1855 until 1873, when he resigned to become Vice-President. [110]

Fernando Wood of New York, Mayor of New York City. [51]

William L. Yancey of Alabama, chairman of the Commission sent to Europe in behalf of the Confederate cause in 1861. [60]

27572

E
440.5
D55

THE DIARY OF A PUBLIC MAN.

DATE DUE

GAYLORD   PRINTED IN U.S.A.